cover: Alban Barré

thanks to: Solal Guyon-Barré, Stephan May, Gilles Barbier, Nathalie Valois, Galerie GP & N Valois, Pierre Giner, Eric Chevillard, éditions de Minuit, Lynne Cohen, Olga Korper Gallery, Fabienne Leclerc, In Situ, Musée des beaux-arts du Canada, Pia Rönicke, GB Agency et Andersen's, Copenhaguen, Alexandra Theiler Furrer, Philippe Garrel, Mathieu Briand, Alban Barré, Magali Guyon, Christophe Hanna, Al Dante, Michelangelo Antonioni, Thomas Demand, Esther Schipper Gallery, Toshio Iwaï, Kolkoz, Galerie Emmanuel Perrotin, Tobias Bernstrup, Cosmic Galerie, Felix Stephan Huber, Virginie Barré, Stéphane Sautour, Alexandra Schillinger, Galerie Loevenbruck, Cory Arcangel, Jessy Leydier, galerie Thaddaeus Ropac, Gus Van Sant, Alain Resnais, David Fincher, Raoul Ruiz, Christopher Nolan, Peter Greenaway, Mike Figgis, Guillaume Paris, Pandaxpress, Scott McCloud, Davis Foster Wallace, Marion Mazauric, éditions Au Diable Vauvert.

1 CITÉ RIVERIN
75010 PARIS

http://www.disvoir.com

ISBN 2-914-563-30-2
EAN 9782914563307

PRINTED IN EUROPE

NARRATIVITY:
HOW VISUAL ARTS, CINEMA AND LITERATURE ARE TELLING THE WORLD TODAY

RENÉ AUDET

CLAUDE ROMANO

LAURENCE DREYFUS

CARL THERRIEN

HUGUES MARCHAL

Translated from the French by

Paul Buck & Catherine Petit

Edité avec le concours du Ministère Français chargé de la Culture - Centre National du Livre (aide à la traduction).

This translation was published with the aid of the Ministère Français chargé de la Culture - Centre National du Livre.

complete online catalog: http://www.disvoir.com

series edited by
DANIELE RIVIERE

in the same series "visuals arts/ essay"

BLACK IS A COLOR: A HISTORY OF AFRICAN AMERICAN ART
Elvan Zabunyan

KEEP THIS SEX OUT OF MY SIGHT
Elvan Zabunyan, Chrystel Besse, Arlette Fontan, Françoise Gaillard, Marie-Joseph Bertini

CONTEMPORARY PRACTICES: ART AS EXPERIENCE
Paul Ardenne, Pascal Beausse, Laurent Goumarre

TECHNO : AN ARTISTIC AND POLITICAL LABORATORY OF THE PRESENT
Michel Gaillot, Jean-Luc Nancy, Michel Maffesoli

SOUND AND THE VISUAL ARTS
Jean-Yves Bosseur

IN FAVOUR OF TODAY'S ART
François Dagognet

CLEMENT GREENBERG BETWEEN THE LINES
Thierry de Duve

SUMMARY

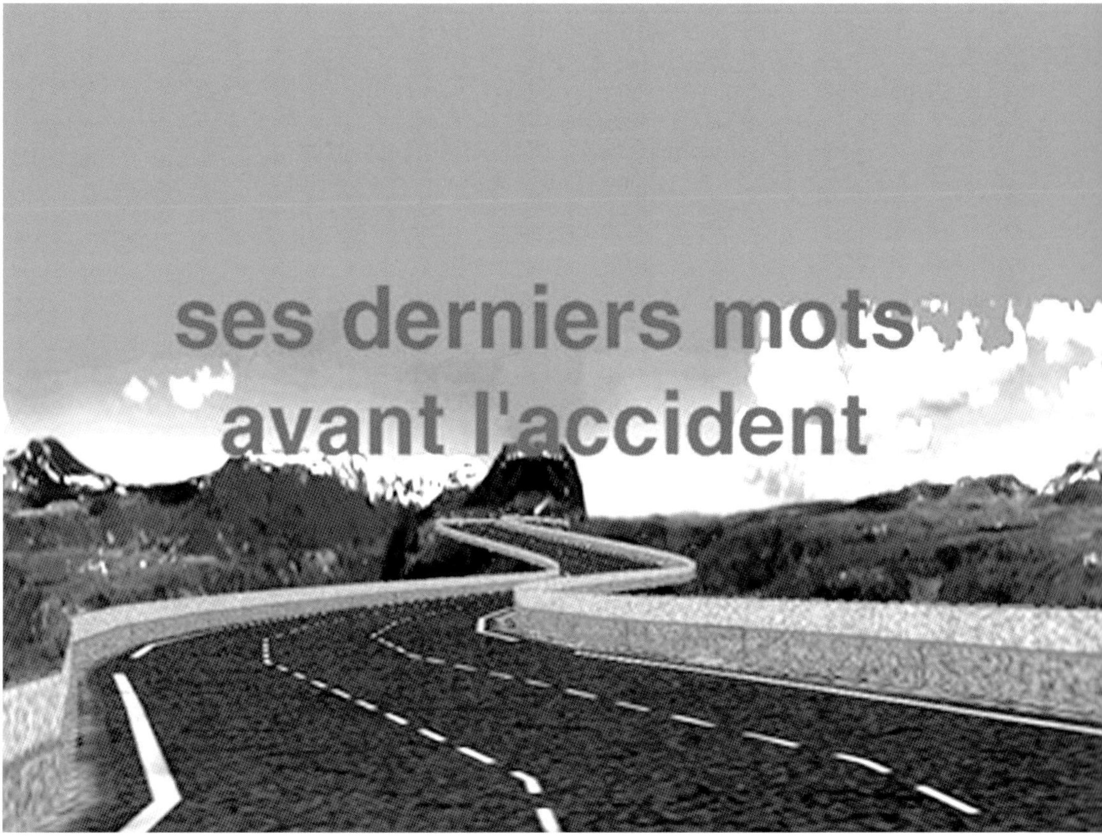

Keep the distance, Pierre Giner, 2002

NARRATIVITY: AWAY FROM STORY, CLOSE TO EVENTNESS

I want to say I may have seen my son die this morning.

As a starting point *in medias res*, this opening sentence of the well-known hypertextual fiction, *Afternoon, a story*, by Michael Joyce, is everything but the beginning of a narrative. By declaiming from the onset that affirmation showing his lacunar perception, the character-narrator places the text he constructs in a state of uncertainty. The event which forms the argument, the original structure of the anecdote is quite possibly a *non-event*. It seems difficult, in the circumstances, to pretend to the setting up of a narrative around that virtuality—a matter of fact that is confirmed by the exploration of that fiction on numerical support. In reality, by always deferring the moment of verification of that fleeting vision, when he would have seen his wife and son involved in a serious car accident, the narrator jams the mechanics of the narrative. Blocking the possible unfolding of the actions, preventing the chain of causality from being established, from revealing itself, it forces the reader to get lost in palavers—hypotheses, projections and narrative loops—that the hypertextual support conveys with a feeling of disorientation perfectly adapted to the purpose of the fiction.

That intentional dissolution of the narrative, based on the denial of the event, is mainly observed—an unimaginable source of frustration—in the absence of a closure, of a resolution of the tension set in place by those very first words however endowed with an unquestionable effectiveness. Even if the protagonist reflects upon the fact that "There is an end to everything, to any mystery," the hyperfiction *Afternoon* doesn't close in the manner of a conventional novel. The reader is urged to wear away, his impatience or frustration leading him to shut down the computer screen of his own free will. If by chance the reader lands on that page declaring that to everything there is an end, he can read a screen page set forth by a meta-narrator (the author?) who gives his opinion on the idea of narrative closure: "Closure is, as in any fiction, a suspect quality, although here it is made manifest. When the story no longer progresses, or when it cycles, or when you tire of the paths, the experience of reading it ends." By stating that exhaustion (of the fictional matter, anyway), the meta-narrator retorts that it is not absolute: by inviting the reader to re-start his journey in hyperfiction, he insists here on the multivocal dimension of words, there on the forking intrinsic to the actions possible (in the Borges fashion), leaving fresh opportunities to be read. That plunging into fiction is evidently constructed to the detriment of a setting up of the narrative, here dissolved in the shattering of a hypertext and in the uncertainty of the event.[1]

Though it is obviously a non-narrative, does that text prevent, for all that, a complete recognition of its fundamental narrative character? Does one talk about the same thing when one talks about a narrative as the foundation of a work and the narrative dimension that characterizes that prose? Is the narrativity of a text summed up in the presence of a narrative that structures it? Notional uses and definitions obviously remain to be clarified.

* * *

The omnipresence of the narrative—in our artistic practices and in everyday speech—is one of the most obvious common places, a fact that we won't contest here. The narrative discourse is the founder of fantasies and beliefs, a mode of communication between people, a way to understand transformations through time. It structures the spirit and language, giving to facts and circumstances a way of writing down human memory. Retrospectively, one is hardly surprised that that type of discourse has fascinated to such a degree the twentieth century researchers who have devoted to it a phenomenal amount of explanatory hypotheses, propositions of definition and analytical work. From Vladimir Propp and his typology to the cognitivists and sociolinguists, from Sigmund Freud to the structuralists, historians and philosophers, numerous researchers have tried to seize, in their own way, what is at the basis of that modality of language affixed to human temporality and what makes its singularity compared to other more paradigmatic modes of cognition.

[1] For an attentive analysis to the narratologic features in the hyperfiction *Afternoon*, see Walker (1999).

The results of those investigations, at times complementary, at times contradictory, have been more or less successful, standing out here through the bringing to light of a determining aspect (the enlightening work of Paul Ricœur on temporality), revealing there, afterwards, confusing methodological means (a too canonizing or too specific definition of an artistic practice). The will to lift the conceptual mist surrounding the narrative has often led to a multiplication of angles by which one seizes that linguistic phenomenon—in the circumstances a multiplication of notions, processes, shutters, which can clarify an aspect, or interfere with the elaboration of the narrative: let's refer, as example, to the notions of fabula and subject [sjuzet] (inherited from the Russian formalists), the actants, the narrators/narratees and the focalizers (Greimas, Genette...), not to mention the imperfect correspondences between the terms in different languages (plot, story, narrative / intrigue, histoire, récit). That explosion in terminology, though it bears witness to an effervescence of the reflection on that type of discourse, has scarcely taken shape in the common discourse, except that of literary critics who have adopted the most useful and loquacious tools (those of narratology by Genette, especially). This common discourse, the speech of ordinary people whose only experience of literature is that of a relaxing read, remains based on the most general notions: narrative, story, character. Such an apprehension of the narrative, intuitive and visual, constantly interferes with a more strata-like analysis of the phenomenon, in spite of the scientific character associated with the theoretical discourse of the narrative.

In this context, it is not rare to quote terms according to their general acceptance; in extensive analyses of a body of work or practice, some conceptual gaps slide in, which result in an unfortunate theoretical ambiguity. The most obvious case (which I shall deal with here) is that of the wide use of the term "narrative". Generally taken as synonymous with a work in narrative prose, narrative is used to describe realities that only partially correspond to it. Accused of all the evils in contemporary literature especially—from its misrepresentation to its obliteration, if not its disappearance—it has to take sole charge of the discursive type on which it is built, as well as of the generic practices which it characterizes. That transversal use (or, to be more scathing, that *vicious* use) of the narrative is responsible for improper characterizations or reflections, to which it seems important to bring some light, as modest as that is. The point is here not to launch into a police investigation—what Marie-Laure Ryan also refuses to do in her entry to the word "Narrative" in the *Routledge Encyclopedia of Narrative Theory* (2005)—but rather to push a reflection forward a little further than Ryan has proposed, who falls back on a *fuzzy-set hypothesis* to try to conciliate all the uses of the term (*narrative* being more multivocal than the French *récit* and *narratif*).[2] The example of the hyperfiction, *Afternoon, a story*, given at the beginning of this essay, explicitly illustrates the necessity for the re-reading of terms and accepted meanings however as common as *le récit* and *le narratif*, without for all that giving way to a fuzzy and non-working vision of those notions.

In that sense, this text is for me an opportunity to develop an exploratory proposition which is presented in two steps. The first step consists in taking note of the double dimension of what one generally designates as narrative, meaning the narrative and the narrativity. Those two notions, close but distinct, must then be understood in their respective field of validity; two notions to explain, jointly while still distinguishing one from the other. From several examples, in the continuity of that brief presentation of Michael Joyce's hypertext, I will attempt a differentiation in order to reach a reformulation that will be the least ambiguous possible, as it remains difficult—and certainly incoherent—to completely separate those notions. Some propositions offered in recent years to define the central components of the narrative will be examined in order to throw some light on the confusion brought on by the proximity of those notions. This first step aims thus at distinguishing between narrative and narrativity, the latter being defined indirectly in relation to the narrative which will be replaced in a stricter use than the one which is given to it in common speech. It is from the question: "what story is told in that work?" that we will approach that initial phase.

The second step of that exploration aims more particularly at defining the notion of narrativity. Starting from a reclassifying of the narrative, we will try to apprehend the governing idea which underlines it: my hypothesis is that narrativity is based on the notion of event. If we can intuitively associate the actions (which are the base of the narrative) to a wide conception of eventness, we will rather construct that definition against the common model of the representation of actions, on behalf of a more phenomenological perspective: the narrative is based on the fact that there is an event (and not on an ensemble of countable events). That general setting will lead us to identify in the end three possible orders of event which could induce a narrative character to a work: an

[2] "Should we design a definition that acts like a semantic police, excluding all 'illegitimate' uses of the term 'narrative', but also endangering its theoretical vitality, or should we bow to current fashion, and work out a definition that accepts all current interpretations, at the price of losing some crucial distinction between narrative and other forms or products of mental activity? A compromise between these two possibilities is to regard narrative as a fuzzy set defined at the center by a solid core of properties, but accepting various degrees of membership, depending on which properties a candidate displays." (Ryan, 2005: 345)

inworld event (the easiest to conceive); a discursive event (which acts like a guarantee to the discourse); an operal event (where the event is a result of the textual or artistic device). The objective of that second step is therefore to reach a non-scalar conception of narrativity (as proposed by Gerald Prince, among others), which invites us to evaluate the degree of presence in a text, but rather to approach the narrativity in its various manifestations and in its role in the construction of a work. The convocation (or production) of an event irradiating at the heart of the work, as a pretext allowing *to make happen*, forms a new reading of the narrative fact, which goes beyond the functional approach of the narrative proposed by the heirs of structuralism and which perceives differently the temporal paradigm put forward by White and Ricœur especially.

NARRATIVE AND NARRATIVITY: WHAT STORY?

If it's generally accepted, in literary studies, that the narrative has been badly damaged by the experimentations of the Sixties and Seventies—in France, the *Nouveau Roman*, and in the United States, Postmodernism, without mentioning the textualist movement in a large part of the Western world—the contemporary discourse on literature tends to note the "return of the narrative" which seems to re-assure readers (and, consequently, publishers). The return to a more limpid prose, the setting up of a fiction which does not make transgression its guiding principle, the renewed pleasure of fabulation: those characteristics frequently mentioned would justify thus a return of the *narrative.* Strange shifting, if there ever was one—for, in addition to coming back to a more accessible literature, easier to read, none of those observations really concerns the narrative dimension of the text. In the same way, the critical discourse seems to go from the Seventies to now, from a criticism of the narrative to a look on the conditions of the possibility of a narrative, as noted by Dominique Viart:

> the criticisms targeting the inevitably simplifying, falsifying, arbitrary, conventional, conservative aspects of the narrative are not out-of-date. I would even say that they have paradoxically become sharper while losing their theoretical radicality. For they used to target essentially the narrative itself, while the questioning is now focused on what is upstream of the narrative. For behind the narrative appears what constitutes it, authorizes it, provokes it, solicits it or allows it. From the most immediate taste for fiction, unfolding of

> an unfettered imaginary, to a desire to talk about oneself or find oneself: these are the representations that direct the narrative. (…) Now those systems of representation have faltered too. (Viart, 1998: 12)

If fictionality and narrativity are intimately linked in the readers' mind, especially because of that fundamental question of representation (today under suspicion), they are nevertheless the distinct components of the romanesque practice (to take the example of the dominant genre). The work of *appeasing* of the style and formal processes, if I may say, which characterizes contemporary writing, is certainly not the sure sign of a subjection of the text to the canonic model of the narrative. How to explain then that disguising, in the discourse, of the readable under the label of narrative? Easy solution, quite clearly, because of the important extension of the term—all the more for the narrative often appears inappropriate to describe contemporary artistic practices. It is there that is situated the evidence of a gap between the objects and the discourse which tries to seize them from that common conception of the narrative. To support this evidence, a few recent examples whose problematic character invites us to a new reflection on narrative are presented here, albeit briefly.

• Contemporary fictions frequently fall back on the daily routine of contemporary life to try to express at times a state of being, at others a malaise facing the loss of identity (surmodernity), the difficulty to live in our time or according to one's own values. It is the urban context, as in several contemporary artistic productions, which is used as interface to that malaise in *Dare mo shiranai (Nobody Knows),* a film by the Japanese director Hirokazu Kore-eda. Reporting on a year in the life of four children confined to their Tokyo apartment, the film unfolds with the expectation of Keiko's return, the mother on the run (work, love), and the responsibility the children take on themselves, the responsibility she should assume. Left on their own, more or less clandestine occupants of a tiny apartment, they take one day at a time, living their daily life on the fringes of society. Akira, the oldest, tries to keep alive, if not to ensure, the survival of his brother and sisters, unable to count on the mother's presence. The film, modeled on the four seasons lived in the children's company, follows the consequences of an absence: accumulation of the moments spent waiting, of make-shift solutions for eating and having a roof over their head; transgression of the rules imposed (the escapades out of the apartment, especially); a chronological construction in which the actions of one day have a consequence the following day. That daily life is filled with anecdotes, typically innocuous conflicts between kids and the passing of the stages of growing up.

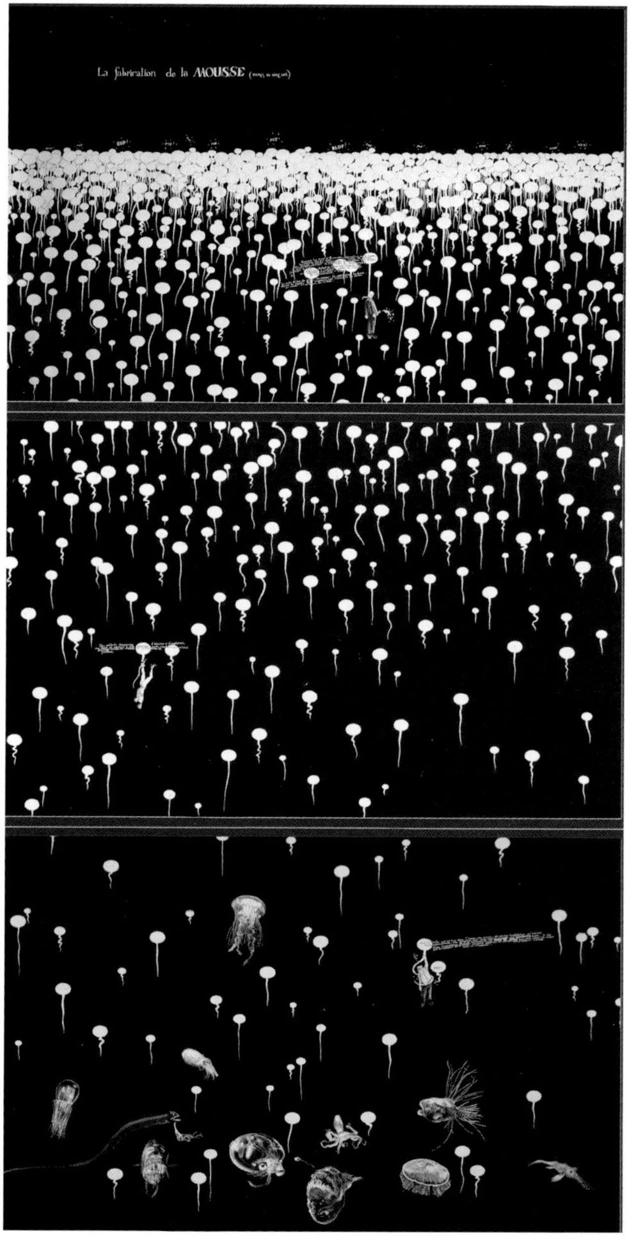

Untitled (bubble making), Gilles Barbier, 2005 - Gouache on paper,
3 parts: each 120 x 190 cm—Private collection, Greece; Courtesy Galerie GP & N Vallois, Paris

Transformations follow the course of the days, with no other perceptible will of a strong demonstration, just as one can hardly imagine that this visual presentation of daily life could end—except for a return of the mother, except for a disruption of the delicate balance established between the four brothers and sisters. The account of one year in the children's life in Tokyo refuses to be constructed as a narrative, nevertheless the audience is invited to witness their adventures.

• Strong from the experimentations made in the past, from Diderot to the Postmodernists, contemporary literature doesn't hesitate to reflect in the works the gesture of writing itself—even more, to narrate that they narrate (even sometimes to narrate that they don't narrate). If the jacket of Eric Chevillard's *Valiant Little Tailor (Le Vaillant petit tailleur)* retains the generic reference "novel", the reason to justify such a decision certainly doesn't lie in the many adventures that the protagonist is involved in, a writer who decides to appropriate the Brothers Grimm's tale and to re-write it—or simply, to write it.[3] With much irony and many winks, the narrator tries to render a new version of the tale, offering a few bifurcations (which prove to be dead ends), commenting on the gesture of writing and posing as a hero made of the same stuff as the tailor he thinks highly of. If there is actually a story with some action which leads to the change of status of the tailor to that of new king, it is nevertheless situated inside a first plot, that of the writer, which is not necessarily marked by exciting adventures. Constructing his work, he comments, shows himself to advantage and offers some reflections on literature. The interest of that *novel* lies instead in the gesture of the retaking of a well-known tale, in the discourse held by the narrator and his exploitation of a narrative plot which is not his own.

• If today one maintains the association of the narrative possibility of photography to what Henri Cartier-Bresson used to call the "decisive moment", it remains however difficult to bring every narrative emanating from a silver print into the logic of the snapshot. That conception centered on the capture of a critical moment, an *eloquent* situation, is not however out-of-date: it admirably supports the dynamics of the report, which persists in the written press (while the televisual medium has diluted that instantaneousness in a video sequence). One will also notice today a work on the way of taking photographs,

[3] "Better, though, that I stick to my first intention, *The Valiant Little Tailor* will be the title known to all, which was missing from my bibliography. (...) But I notice that, through lack of a canonical text, the valiant little tailor has not acceded to the rank of mythical figure like Oedipus, Don Juan, Faust, and a few others who, however, haven't shown as much aptitude as him. / It is the canonical text of that epic, invoked to unfold like an infinite daydream in the individual and collective imagination that, modestly, suspending for numerous months, years perhaps, the work always in progress of my eager masterpiece, I propose to give to the world." (Chevillard, 2003: 19)

to attempt an exploitation of making a narrative of the images—a lengthening of the time of exposure in order to catch the movement, a sequentialization of photos which gives back (or impresses) a movement to the subjects represented. It is however not those processes which make me mention here the photographic production of Lynne Cohen[4]. Refusing the posture of the decisive moment for that of the "found-object quality" of things (Cohen and Thomas, 2001: 24), that photographer's favorite subjects are places: men's clubs, lecture halls, spas..., whose artificial and inhuman character at first disconcerts the spectators. Marked by emptiness and the absence of all human beings, those images could immediately be associated with a documentary or factual conception of photography: seizing the architecture, the modes, the forms, they seem to capture what is not alive, what negates movement. But, as we can see in her more recent photographs of laboratories and military installations, the places represented are always situated on the edge of the narrative, without however succeeding in doing so: a lecture hall (p.108: the photo "*Lecture Hall 1990*") which offers a board showing the military ranks of central Europe, at the bottom of which lies a small satchel (forgotten? by the teacher or a student?); an odd laboratory (p.95), showing a shower, a dummy illustrating the circulatory system, a MacIntosh SE and the intriguing shadow of a skeleton suspended on an unknown structure; a military installation (p.101: the photo "*Military Installation 1998*") (see all the photos here p.29), which lines the photographer up along a trolley on tracks, on which is installed a dummy ready to undergo an experiment (not to say a torture)... Those places, often revelatory of human behavior (through the choice of the shaping of the space available), are particularly charged: "hiding the implausible stories (that the photos) seem to tell" (28), they invite the spectator to get involved in the *reading* of the images, especially by "discovering (in them) the clue of an activity which has just ended or is about to begin" (26). It is on the mode of virtuality that the narrative operates in Cohen's photographic work.

It is obvious that those artistic practices escape the labeling "narrative". Obliteration of the plot, shifting of the representation, virtualization of the possibilities of the making into a narrative: the intuitive designation of those works as being the carriers of stories, appears, after a brief examination, rather unsatisfactory. Facing that fact, one has to wonder about the presuppositions

[4] For a glimpse at that production, see her site: http//www.lynne-cohen.com. The photographs evoked in that text are all reproduced in the exhibition catalogue, *No Man's Land* (the page numbers refer to Cohen and Thomas, 2001). Three reproductions have been attached to this text, courtesy of the photographer. I wish to thank her warmly for her collaboration.

which act in our understanding and our use of the terms narrative and narrativity. Confronted by such disturbing examples, we could be tempted to follow Flaubert when he said that with *Madame Bovary* he was aiming at the ideal of a "book on nothing". In his correspondence with Louise Colet (16 January 1852), he said he wanted to end up with "a book which would have almost no subject matter, or at least where the subject matter would be almost invisible, if that's possible." Though, beginning with a small news item, Flaubert admits that he doesn't give to the novel, *Madame Bovary*, the opportunity to develop around a drama or a strong question—by producing a work with a bearing, with a determining significance through the subject matters it sets up and the actions which animate the characters –, contemporary artists push that shifting even further. Not only do they take away the relevance of the narrative which is the foundation of the work, but on top of that they weaken, if not deconstruct that narrative: those artistic productions do not narrate anything (in the strong sense of the narrative) and, moreover, they refuse to bend to the model of the narrative. Such a way to consider those works, through the rocks they strike, calls for a questioning of the notions of narrative and narrativity.

If the question "what story do those works tell us?" comes immediately to mind, when approaching the three examples cited above, a corollary question is truly that of the definition of the narrative. Presented, in a dictionary of the language, as the process of narrating a story (which is an account of events), that definition gains very little precision in the theoretical books on the subject. Two tendencies can easily be identified, the first favoring a synthetic definition, the second dissecting the components of the narrative. The first generally calls for the idea of a representation of actions, taking its inspiration from, amongst others, Aristotle's *Poetics* (as Molino and Lafhail-Molino remind us (2003): "to represent beings acting". That representation, at the same time process and result, is the foundation of Gerald Prince's proposition in his *Dictionary of Narratology* (2003): "The representation (as product and process, object and act, structure and structuration) of one or more real or fictive events communicated by one, two, or several (more or less overt) narrators to one, two or several (more or less overt) narratees" ("Narrative" entry: 58). The definition proposed by Prince tries to take into serious consideration a series of manifestations and processes underlined by the term "narrative"—like the entry "Narrative" in the *Routledge Encyclopedia of Narrative Theory* (2005), in which, however, Marie-Laure Ryan doesn't resolve in her attempts at an unique definition, trapped by various propositions, multiple perspectives (and thus by contradictory definitions). The perspective that's retained, in that tendency, generally helps to seize the global function of the narrative, meaning that combination of beings and actions, as Molino and Lafhail-Molino sum up, "the narrative staging characters and a story" (2003:22).

The abundance mentioned by Ryan is (partially) dealt with by the definitions of the second tendency: the elements belonging in the production of the narrative are serialized there. Gérard Genette's proposition is probably the most notorious. It is constructed on the acquired attainments of structuralism (for example capitalizing on the advances of Bremond for the interactions of roles during the action, and those of Greimas, in his considering of the textual effects of that actantial dimension) to reach an identification of three constituents of the narrative text. He proposes "to call *story* the signified or narrative content (even though that content finds itself being, in the circumstances, of a weak dramatic intensity or factual tenor), *narrative* the so-called signifying, statement, discourse or narrative text itself, and *narration* the producing narrative act, and, by extension, the ensemble of the real or fictive situation in which it takes place" (1972:72). Genette isolates thus the factual matter (the story, as the chronological series of facts able to be linked in a causal way) from the process supporting the discourse (the narrator as motor of the narration), that putting into words of a matter producing a narrative, the result of the appropriation of a chronological sequence and its plotting.[5] That interaction of three elements is in keeping with a process clearly centered on the production of the narrative and its enunciative functioning.

This double tendency sheds light on the various parts of the complicated question of the definition of narrative (without even covering all the perspectives developed today in order to understand it). In order to propose a beaconed re-reading of that notion, according to its differentiation regarding narrativity, I propose to understand the narrative as the form created from narrativity, as the concrete modality of it (for which I will attempt later to propose a specific definition). Taking up the meaning given to the term by Genette, the narrative would correspond to the text itself in its structuration and its characteristics. If it is the incarnation of narrativity, the narrative must be understood in the rules that govern that form, in its minimal conditions of realization. In order to explore that functional (and strict) conception of the

[5] Paul Ricœur summarizes that appropriation (by removing the transformational connotation) by talking about the conjunction of a sequential dimension and a configurational dimension, "universal trait of every narrative", (1980: 41).

narrative, a few components will be discussed, in the light of the examples proposed earlier—examples that will prove, paradoxically, rather revealing.

If one talks about a narrative, it is because something happens in it. This characterization, based on the **action** is commonly used in the pedagogy of narrative forms (taking up the principles stated by Greimas, especially): the narrative is the support for a modification of state (the final state being different from the initial state). There is a necessary disruption that has to be resolved through a series of interventions, of actions that are operative in the completion of the transformation. According to such a minimal definition of the action, there's no problem in seeing a narrative in *Dare mo shiranai*: a granulated action, spread day after day, allows the passage from the naïve life of the children to a more conscious life (through the learning by experience of the world realities and the dramatic fall of little Yuki). It's already more difficult to understand what is happening in *The Valiant Little Tailor*, because of the discursive and reflexive dimension of the action of the first level. In a way, through that work of interiority which doesn't seem anchored in a plot, one comes closer to what Monika Fludernik designates by *experientiality*, which she resumes as the "quasi-mimetic evocation of 'real-life' experience" (2005:155). That notion echoes a different comprehension of narratives, whose plot's central dimension is reconsidered to the benefit of a taking into account of the experimenting of narration itself (in what it provoked cognitively and emotionally). The discourse, according to that point of view, would account for the mental narrative of the narrator, making obsolete, as a result, the action as structuring principle and the plot which integrates it in the narrative scheme. If one associates straight away that dimension of *experientiality* to the more psychological works, to the romanesque *stream of consciousness* novels of the twentieth century, it appears as much revealing of the dynamics in place in a novel which voluntarily disrupts the conventions of representation (some would say: a Postmodern novel) like *The Valiant Little Tailor.*

Such a shifting, in which the importance of the plot is made relative, clearly displays the fundamental character of the relations existing between the various actions, understood in a broad sense (and that Ryan (1991) classifies in *happenings, actions* and *moves*: I'll come back to that later). These relations come under what we call **teleology,** which corresponds to the strong concretization of the configurational dimension mentioned by Ricœur—or the casuality erected as a system. The construction of a discourse, here a narrative, according to its finality (which sometimes corresponds to the narrative end) results in a tight weaving of the reported actions and their transmission: the efficiency of the narrative, its plot, its interest—its *tellability*, in Ryan's terms[6])—depends on it closely. How to understand then the logics of series and the coherence of those "hidden stories" behind Lynne Cohen's photos? If one postulates a narrative possibility around those images, it is often because of an implicit causality linked to an object, a shadow, an emptiness one is drawn, like spectators, to fill. But from that to actually reconstitute a whole chain of causalities (founder of a whole narrative), there is an abyss one could not leap over. Such a chain seems to run through *Dare mo shiranai*, but the links could here simply be arranged by destiny, chance or fortune, according to the name one gives to that acting force. The actions are linked to one another, unfold rather freely, a consequence of the everydayness which does not have the power of a plot. There are undoubtedly new developments which punctuate the film, moments of tension which give it its force (*peaks and valleys*, as Ryan puts it), but the power of that work is surely to be found in its refusal to close, and thus to free itself from teleological constraint.

Such a modulation of the common acceptance of the plot—which normally has to keep us in suspense to lead us, *in fine*, to a satisfying resolution—appears here rather disturbing. The *emplotment* (to take Hayden White's term), that allows the transmutation of an ensemble of facts, of actions into a story (with a beginning, a development and an end) ends up being badly treated here. Consequently it is the conventional conduct of the action through a narrative which those works attack, and not necessarily their teleological dimension: the finality of representations like those of Cohen or Kore-eda doesn't actually lie in a liberating narrative completion of a tension, but in the demonstration of the impossibility of its resolution[7]. The photographs' aim is to improve the sharpness of the look in the understanding of human behaviors (which are temporally upstream and downstream of the captured places); the everydayness reflected by the film is not submitted to a vectoriality like that developed by the narrative. The principle to which those two artistic

[6] "The study of what makes a narrative successful involves two components: the rhetorical, or performantial component, which focuses on the discourse features through which narrators display storyworld in a way that invites audiences to respond emotionally, intellectually, or aesthetically; and the tellability component, which focuses on the discourse-independent features that predict such responses. Tellability involves a wide variety of principles: context-specific and context-free; culture-relative and universal; semantic and pragmatic. Moreover, tellability can be concentrated in a single, precisely identifiable feature—the point of the text, such as the punch line or the piece of information wanted by the hearer—or it can be the effect of properties that operate throughout the narrative, structuring interest in the story as a sequence of peaks and valleys." (Ryan, 2005: 590)

[7] On the question of the closure of the narrative, see the synthesis offered by Paul Ricœur (1984: 40-58).

productions seem to be submitted is in reality that of **temporality**, so dear to Paul Ricœur in his exploration of the possibilities and stakes of the narrative. To renounce temporality would be to renounce something to happen, would be to no longer consider a before and an after. It seems there is in the relations between temporality and teleology (between temporality and action), all the room necessary to the coming out of the narrative of a work, but without for all of that leaving the field of the narrative. Taking the opposite view of Ricœur, who distinguishes between the rejection of chronology (as structuration of the actions in a work) and the (impossible) rejection of the configuration proper to any narrative (1984: 50-51), I would say that those works tend to get rid of the causality to return to the fundamental pattern of the before-after, which is the mode of primary structuration of the human psyche. By preferring the neutral temporal succession, they seem to poke fun at the *post hoc, ergo propter hoc* sophism (following that, thus because of that): it is not because the actions follow each other that they are determined by one another, but at the same time those works are also the recipient of that sophism: the actions can follow one another and simply link together. So temporality is here perceived in its productive rather than structuring aspect: inscribing the actions in a simple succession, it helps to circumvert the configuration (through the everydayness, through up and down stream) to the benefit of a representation split in its scope, in its significance—in its signifying totality, here pushed back in a virtuality that the reader could choose to invest or to actualize, if his conventional reference points are not shattered too much.

To those three extremely significant components in the comprehension of the narrative are added two others which often go unnoticed, which accompany them without necessarily being identified. It, however, seems to me useful to mention them, in the perspective of a more functional definition of narrativity (in the second part). The first component is that of the narrative **voice**. A dimension studied considerably in literature[8] in recent years, and questioned by cinema experts, the voice refers to the putting into words of the narrative through an intervening authority, the narrator, who fits inside the world represented. What seems interesting here is not so much the incarnation of that voice as its very existence: the narrative must be taken over inside the discourse itself, either by a superior being (an exact copy of the Author, and not a god…) or by a character involved in the diegesis. The implication of this statement is clearly that a narrative

[8] See especially Dominique Rabaté's works.

doesn't narrate itself all by itself. It is the basic argumentation in *The Valiant Little Tailor*, summoned up in the fiction offered and exemplified by the *narrative* on the first level: a writer, who considers that nobody has officially claimed the authorship of the tale, decides to take responsibility for it, to write it, to tell it again. The novel thus exacerbates the gesture of enunciation: disproportionate demonstration, even the grotesque of the writer's position; obvious and strongly underlined digressions; metatextual position, where the commentary on the work is mixed in with the novel, in the course of one sentence:

> Now that time has elapsed, as I turn back on the work accomplished, I think I can say without showing off that I haven't demerited. The narrative has gained in density, in depth, it hasn't lost any of its energy, perhaps it is even more lively now, if not as vivacious as its mischievous hero who, laughing fully, opens wide his door and invites us to come in. / How to refuse? / The old gossip, pressed to conclude a sale which appears to be a bargain, rushes in. (2003: 35-36)

A theatrical voice, that romanesque narration multiplies the traces of an authority that takes on the narrative discourse from inside the fiction.

That relation between representation and discerning subject is very different in the case of photography. The result of a perception, of a *focalization* (to put a common term back into literary narratology), the photographic image constantly bears witness to that enunciation, that capture which is rendered as a singular image. In a way, photography is brought much closer to the cinema through that question of the point of view on an object, a discipline in which a substantial theoretical discourse on those problematics of perception, of taking charge has developed. Let's bring to mind the distinction established by André Gaudreault between *monstration* and *narration*. Roger Odin postulates that that distinction doesn't account for the gesture of the putting into narrative of cinema, of what he calls *narrativisation* (which distinguishes itself "by the inscription of movements in the register of actions and by the production of a feeling of narrativity" (2000:32)—he ends up distinguishing between three types of instances: narrativisor, monstrator and narrator. That trichotomy, useful to understand the cinematic narratives in several shots, seems superfluous for photography, which in reality constitutes a statement in one shot; I however keep that idea of monstrator which, in the world of cinema, "during the shooting, proceeds to the capture of the shots" (Odin, 2000: 26). Incarnation of the look, that monstrator, yet off-camera, seems at times extremely present in Lynne Cohen's works: in that military installation where the camera is at the end

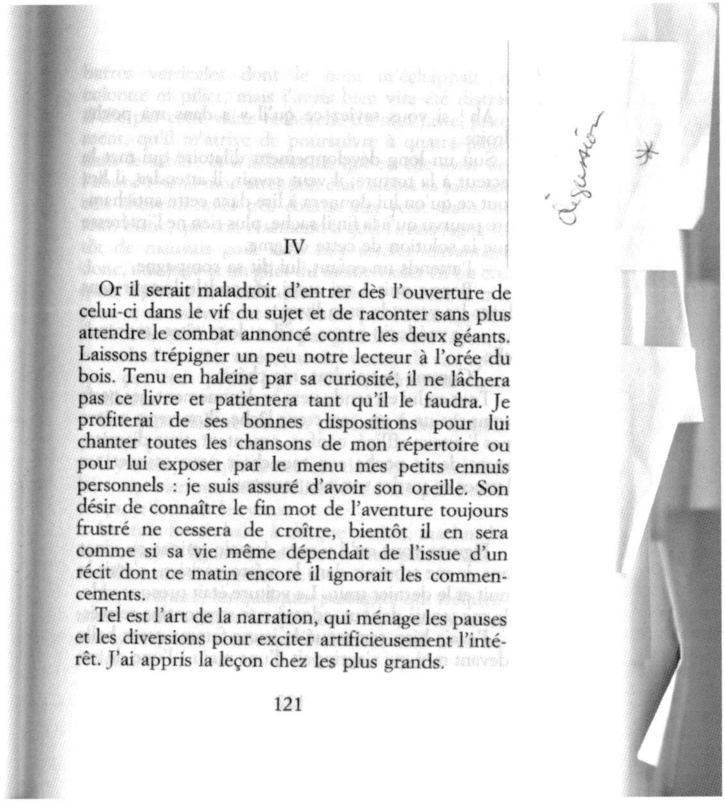

IV

Or il serait maladroit d'entrer dès l'ouverture de celui-ci dans le vif du sujet et de raconter sans plus attendre le combat annoncé contre les deux géants. Laissons trépigner un peu notre lecteur à l'orée du bois. Tenu en haleine par sa curiosité, il ne lâchera pas ce livre et patientera tant qu'il le faudra. Je profiterai de ses bonnes dispositions pour lui chanter toutes les chansons de mon répertoire ou pour lui exposer par le menu mes petits ennuis personnels : je suis assuré d'avoir son oreille. Son désir de connaître le fin mot de l'aventure toujours frustré ne cessera de croître, bientôt il en sera comme si sa vie même dépendait de l'issue d'un récit dont ce matin encore il ignorait les commencements.

Tel est l'art de la narration, qui ménage les pauses et les diversions pour exciter artificieusement l'intérêt. J'ai appris la leçon chez les plus grands.

121

Le Vaillant petit tailleur (The Valiant Little Tailor), by the french writer Eric Chevillard, ed. de Minuit, 2004 p.121

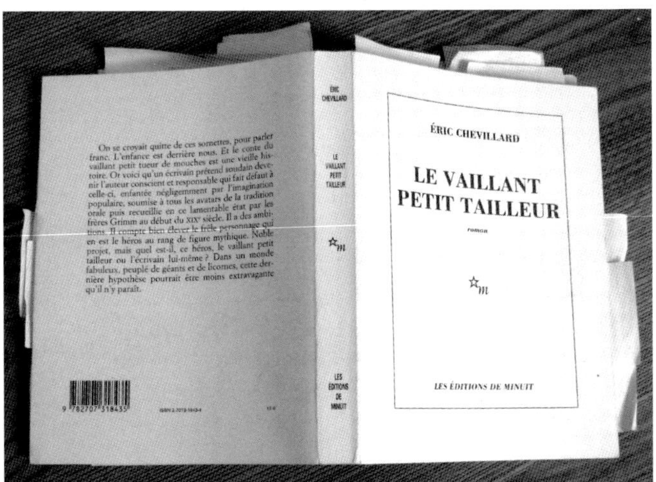

of the track, in that other (p.98) where the light illuminating the room seems to come from behind the photographer, in a police shooting gallery (p.57) where the camera almost plays with the barrel before shooting. That inscription of the look in the photo, indirectly potent, shows participation to the representation, an implication in the establishment of conditions minimal to the emerging of narrative fragments. The question of the voice, so linguistically defined in literature, drifts towards the question of the point of view (as much as full of possibilities in narratology) when the time comes to account for the perceptual dynamism in photography.

The last factor implicit in the characterization of a narrative is that of the assignation of the **subject** implicated in the actions. The literary works in which that variable is significatively problematized are rare: even in allegoric texts, a subject fits in a series of actions, whatever its nature—since the allegory is precisely the transposition of a human subject into another entity (animal, etc) or, on the opposite, an abstract notion placed in a scheme of actions proper to a human subject. It is more in cinematic[9] productions and in photography that this assignation of actions can appear problematic. In Lynne Cohen's photos, no human subject, not even a living being is represented; at best, some dummies (or bits of dummies) add an anthropomorphic face to those places stripped of all life. However, in spite of that absence, many elements call for a human presence which could manifest itself: the case forgotten in the lecture hall, the number of seats (in the offices, in the spas), tools in the laboratories—without counting the inscriptions ("PLAY AT YOUR OWN [RISK]" in a game of war (p.65) and a window, through which one can see trees, where a person, found in that very cold laboratory, could stare blankly. (p.110: the photo "*Laboratory 1999*"). The virtuality of a narrative in those photographs lies in the imminence of an action, which makes possible the projection of a subject in those places however empty, at the moment of the capture of the image, of any human presence.

Action, teleology, temporality, voice, subject: those five components define the narrative and allow it to happen. A subject involved in actions whose organization (temporal and configurational) is produced by an instance internal to the fiction: here is a way to synthesize, to excess surely, the beaconing of the narrative. All those components, as we have seen, can be questioned, modulated, perverted through artistic works. The resultant will often be that the reader, the spectator, will wonder about the presence of the narrative: does it escape when one tries to reconstitute it? Does it seem aporetic? Are its mechanisms widely

[9] However, even docu-fictions like *Microcosmos* (Nunidsany and Pérennou, 1960) are focused on subjects.

exposed to view? Does it obey a logic different to that of the plot? The frequent evidences of those questionings when one approaches contemporary works—questionings, and sometimes even signs of confusion or perplexity—illustrate rather well the out of touch character of the term "narrative" to designate those artistic productions. Nevertheless, it often remains difficult to renounce acknowledging in them an analogy with the narrative, to feel in their contact, to take up Odin's formula, a *feeling of narrativity*. It seems useful, at the end of that beaconing of the narrative as a practice, to question now the definition of narrativity and its operativity in the description of some contemporary works.

NARRATIVITY: A MINIMAL NARRATIVE OR A RETURN TO EVENTNESS[10]?

Often the notion of narrativity, in normal speech, is used as a synonym of narrative (or else, an expression so close that one echoes the other: the "narrativity of a text" evokes the fact that it is a narrative, and vice versa). The examination of several propositions of definition of that expression is quite surprising: while the English-speaking researchers confront the difficulty represented by that task, their French-speaking colleagues seem to take it for granted, so much is the notion generally mistaken for that of the narrative[11] or plainly ignored by the theoretical books and dictionaries of literary terms.[12] The relationship intimately inscribed in the root of the words, in the English language, to designate the characteristics of the discourse and its realization (*narrativity* and *narrative*) perhaps explains their undifferentiated use, when the label of *récit* seems to call with less urgency the one, rarer it's true, of *narrativité* even though both are constantly mistaken for one another. Why thus that additional notion? How to justify it?

[10] The term "eventness" has been coined here to act as an equivalent to the French word "événementialité"; in the same way, "event" is used for "événement", even if the English word comes with many connotations that cannot be ignored.

[11] Thus the entry for "narrativity" in Louis Armantier's *Dictionnaire de la théorie et de l'histoire littéraires du XIXe siècle à nos jours* dodges the question by referring to the definition proposed by Mieke Bal in the opening of *Narratologie*, where she mentions that narrativity "is the way the text is decoded like narrative. So one can say that narrativity is determined by the relations between the narrative text, the narrative and the story" (1986: 211).

[12] The exceptions are bewildering. Wondering about the "pre-requisite and *sine qua non* conditions for an object to be narrative", Gérard-Denis Parcy ends up postulating that "as there are several narratologies, there are several narrativities", after which he carries out a surprising shift between genre and discursive type: "But curiously enough narratology *stricto sensu* hasn't claimed its which is however obvious. We would have liked it to tell us in black and white that it concerns the specificity of the novel, based on the relations between story, narration and narrative, and on a complex play on modalities". (1971: 71)

Approaching the question is generally distinguishing between narrativity as a form of text[13] and narrativity as discursive variable of that text. Gerald Prince was one of the first to venture in that direction. His *Dictionary of Narratology* shows that double meaning of the term: "The set of properties characterizing narrative and distinguishing it from non-narrative; the formal and contextual features making a (narrative) text more or less narrative, as it were." (Prince, 2003: 65) That fracture is constantly echoed by various theoreticians, starting with himself, who takes it up again in the entry for "Narrativity", in the *Routledge Encyclopedia of Narrative Theory* (2005: 387-388), where he opposes "the quality of being narrative" (which can be evaluated through various properties, like the temporal organization of actions) and "the set of optional features that make narrative more prototypically narrative-like". In order to distinguish between those two dimensions, one frequently associates the term *narrativehood* to the first meaning, while *narrativity* is reserved for the second; the first "is usually considered a matter of kind (texts are narrative or they are not)", and the second "a matter of degree", some narratives being more narrative than others. Amongst the factors allowing the evaluation of that degree of narrativity, one mentions the presence of a story which represents a whole made of interconnected situations, which lies on a conflict having a meaning from a human point of view. That dichotomous model is taken up by David Herman, whose semi-cognitive perspective seems compatible with such a reading of narrativity.[14] Besides, he brings back to mind the distinction established between tellability and narrativity (in its scalar meaning), the first lingering on the configurations of facts, the second on the sequences integrating those configurations of facts. We will notice here that narrativity is already instinctively connected to the general movement within a narrative.

Marie-Laure Ryan tries to detach herself from that somehow embarrassing (and little effective) definition (the two dimensions calling each other), by

[13] This is also the starting point of a proposition for the definition of narrativity, that of Greimas and Courtés in their *Dictionnaire raisonné de la théorie du langage / Sémiotique*. Starting from the idea of a property of the discourse that allows the distinction between the narrative discourses and the non-narrative discourses, they quickly drift away towards the characterization of that narrative discourse (enunciative questions, types of structures present in a text). The falling point is nevertheless surprising, narrativity being brought back to its fundamental function as the producer of meaning: "In the semiotic project which is ours, generalized narrativity—freed from its restrictive sense which linked it to the figurative forms of the narratives—is considered as the organizing principle of all discourse." (1979: 249)

[14] "capturing the difference between narratives and stereotyped sequences of events or scripts is tantamount to defining *narrativehood*, or what makes a story a story. Capturing the variable quality of this contrast—that is, accounting for the way different kinds of narratives orient themselves differently toward stereotyped sequences of actions and events—is tantamount to defining *narrativity*, or how readily a narrative can be processed *as* a narrative." (2002: 86)

proposing instead a modal conception of narrativity. In the conclusion of her book, *Possible Worlds, Artificial Intelligence, and Narrative Theory*, she opens up the reflection when she proposes to distinguish between literal narrativity and figured narrativity (1991: 265-266), though from the only case of textual narrativity. She goes back on that proposition—and on that mediatic restriction—in an article (1992) where she presents a paper with a dozen possible modes of narrativity, among which, *simple, complex, braided, diluted, embryonic, underlying, deferred...* She observes straight away the restrictive conception of narrativity which postulated a narrator narrating (thus a text and a fictionalized enunciating instance), to turn to a more open conception, in which the narrativity would be guided by three principles: the setting up of a world (and characters inhabiting it), the occurrence of changes of state implying actions inscribed in a temporal sequence, and the possibility of identification of a network of aims, causal relations and motivations which assure the coherence of the plot. The exploration of identified modes quickly leads to notice that there are not types of narrativity, but rather types of uses, of creation of the narrative: Ryan recognizes the formal dimension of that categorization, but also adds to them a phenomenological dimension, in which the reader's look through the narrative is taken into account. It nevertheless remains that Ryan's proposition projects a conception of narrativity copied from the textual realization which constitutes the narrative—which the sub-categorization put forward as a conclusion shows, that one distinguishing the modes which propose a "full realization of narrativity" from those which imply "a deficient manifestation".

What emerges from that terminological crossing is really to what degree the conception of the plot remains strongly anchored in the discourse bearing on all narrative manifestation. The detachment from the narrative, from its definitional parameters remains in these propositions the most minimal, as if *narrative* and *narrativity* overlapped each other perfectly, as if the use of the narrative type was enough to recognize in it a narrative, as if that use couldn't happen outside what is formalized as a narrative. In his "rereading" of the notion of narrativity, Gerard Prince ends up saying it explicitly: "What narrativity seems primarily linked to is general narrative configuration (as opposed to specific thematic traits, contextual pointedness, or textual value). More particularly, it seems linked to the formal nature of the narrated (e.g., structural closure), that of the narrating (e.g., foregrounding of event discreteness) and the relations between the two (e.g., no inordinate amounts of commentary)." (1999: 48) That strong anchorage in the fundamental characteristics of the narrative also finds its echo in the French-speaking field; let's take for example the linguistic propositions of Jean-Michel Adam (2001), whose approach of the narrative discourse (his "prototype of the narrative sequence") reflects almost identically the narrative considered on the scale of a whole text. If one only reads the theoretical books on narrative theory, one would end up believing that narrativity is what helps to validate, for a text, its designation as "narrative", that the type of discourse called "narrative" is necessarily created in the form of a narrative.

The first half of this text, however, has showed how interferences, diverging constructions of the discourse and semiological characteristics can push aside the narrative without, for that matter, preventing a form of narrative realization of the work. The experience of artistic practices (contemporary, but also baroque and modern) constantly prompts us to think that there is an error (probably of structuralist origin) in the fact of superimposing narrative and narrativity—as shown in our discomfort, our dissatisfaction with describing the process of narrative in certain works, because we always base our perception on that narrative, a totaling form of narrativity incarnated in a medium. So it seems advisable, in such a context, to slightly modulate that conception of narrativity in order to make it more efficient.

That modulation mainly consists in the broadening of the notion of narrativity, so as to detach it from its realization in the form of a narrative—which possesses its specific characteristics and rules. In separating oneself from the concrete manifestation that the narrative constitutes, one has to go back to the basic principle, to try to grasp the phenomenon at the heart of narrativity. The work of *expurgation* imposed by the examination of the three works mentioned earlier (which in their own way were detached from the narrative as such) suggests that I put forward the notion of event. Its French equivalent, *événement*, is barely used to explain the narrative functioning of a work. However the word *event* is more often employed. Used to designate the entirety of possible types of actions of a narrative, the *event* is associated with a change of state ("a change of state manifested in discourse by a process statement in the mode of *Do* or *Happen*" (Prince 2003: 28)). So, according to the system of dividing proposed by Seymour Chatman, it covers *actions* (intentional gestures) and *happenings* (what happens accidentally, by dint of nature or chance).[15] As a motor of the changing of states, the *events* are not considered sufficient to produce narratives,

[15] Ryan (1991) clarifies that proposition by distinguishing the *happenings* from the *actions* (which can be, in a more specific way, *moves*—actions "with a high-priority goal and a high risk of failure" (130)).

as Herman reminds us (2005: 151) by underlying the necessity for a structure, a configuration integrating states and *events* to form a plot. I suggest using the word "event" in a broader sense; it thus takes here another connotation, referring to each act which could have an effect on things unfolding.

This structuralist conception of the event very closely echoes Iouri Lotman's propositions in *La structure du texte artistique* (1973), in which he argues the place of the event in the construction of the subject (a common but ambiguous translation of *sjuzet*, whose closest equivalent would be "plot"). Lotman is in keeping with the same tendency: he uses the notion of event to describe the various actions locatable in a work. So he declares that "the event is taken for the smallest unity, indissoluble from the construction of the subject" (324), to then bring into play the degree of inclusion of the notion: "the event can be understood as a hierarchy of events of more particular levels, like a chain of events, meaning as a subject" (326). However, his presentation of the definition of the event and the relation he establishes between that event and its context seem to me to shed light on another level. Mentioning that "the event in the text is the movement of the character through the border of the semantic field" (326), he really shows the exceptional character of what's happening—he reminds us, on page 327, that the existence itself of the event depends on a non-respect of the norm, of a departure from the ordinary. It is thus through the violation of the space assigned to him that the character produces an event. And the main quality of that event is consequently its virtuality: "The event is considered as what happened at the same time as what could have not happened." (330) Recalling the (narrative) value of the event, its interest in the dynamics between the narrator and his interlocutor, Lotman clearly positions himself in a dynamics of tellability (what deserves to be narrated? what is interesting enough to be narrated?). It is however on those questions of the virtuality and the departure from the ordinary that I'll pursue here my exploratory reflection on narrativity.

In order to base my exploration around the notion of event, I shall borrow a few propositions drawn from *L'événement et le monde*, a philosophical reading of that notion made by Claude Romano (1999). He works on the fundamental definition of the event, which rests on a series of phenomenological references useful to its understanding (see the first part of the book). From those observations, I shall consider a few. First, the event is a change that occurs, something *happens (advient)*. To be more precise, Romano goes back to the etymology of the word: "event" (événement)" comes from the Latin *evenire*,

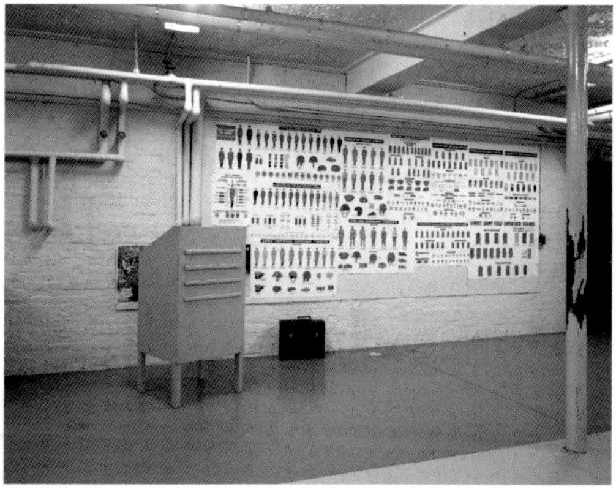

Lecture Hall 1990 - Gelatin silver print - 111x129 cm
Courtesy Olga Korper Gallery, Toronto

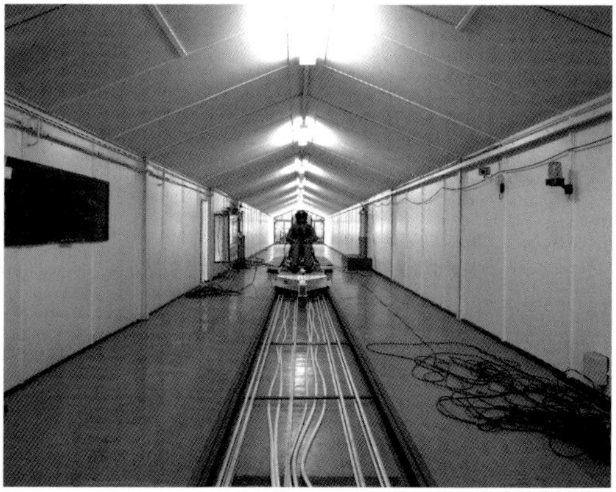

Military installation 1998 - Gelatin silver print - 111x129 cm
Courtesy In Situ Fabienne Leclerc, Paris

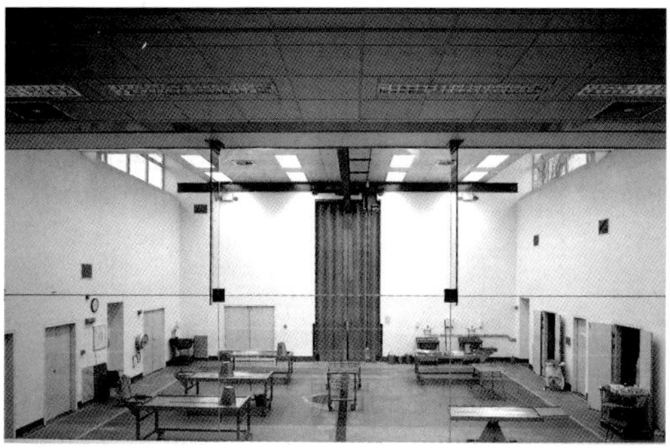

Laboratory 1999 - Dye coupler print - 111x136.6 cm
Courtesy Collection Musée des beaux-arts du Canada, Ottawa

which means not only "to happen", "to occur", "to take place," "to accomplish", but also "*to befall*"*: alicui, to someone.*" (44-45). The fact becomes event when it's assigned: it carries meaning, in a given context, for an *advenant* (a subject to whom something can happen). "*The event is nothing but that impersonal reconfiguration of my possibles and the world which occurs in a fact and through which it opens a gap into my own adventure.*" (45): it is the out of norm, out of the ordinary characteristic already mentioned by Lotman, which brings a disruption for someone, a change in an otherwise stable and predictable state.

From that conception of the event I'll keep the *fulgurating* character—referring here to the most concrete manifestation of that fulgurance to echo Romano's canonical example of the lighting which gleams. It is that sudden emergence, that disruption of an environment that matters to me here: the event is the pivotal moment around which the feeling of narrativity is built, to quote Roger Odin's beautiful formula. That action in which, following Ricœur, he acknowledges the potential for a story,[16] perfectly corresponds to such a concept of the event, a better chosen word, with less connotation than the word "action", it seems to me, to designate the moment when everything topples over—and to evoke the virtuality of what can be built following that sudden appearance. Romano talks accurately about the *passability* (33) of the happening, that opening to what can happen; I shall add that the event itself is characterized by that passability, in the fact that it opens itself to a transformation which goes beyond the simple fact which constitutes it. From there, I think, a proximity is woven between the incident and that potentiality of the action talked about by Odin, between the event and the construction of the narrative feeling through the *disnarrated*, the micro-narratives which do not exist, the roads not taken by the characters (designated as such by Gerald Prince, but specified by Ryan (1991)). The narrative virtuality underlying any narrative lies thus in that fundamental characteristic of the event, at the root of narrativity.

What allows us to see in the event that narrative potentiality? Beyond that virtuality, what invites the acknowledgement of a narrativity? One could bring on here the notion of *montrance* that Romano borrows from Claudel. "It is only by virtue of its presence that the event can precisely emerge with the 'independence' which is its own in regard to any typically human 'doing'; (…) that it can be rigorously 'phenomenon', if the phenomenon is what shows itself from itself, *as itself*" (42), which is referred to by the German word *Erscheinung*

[16] "It is out of question to take up, here, in detail, Paul Ricœur's analyses (…), I will simply remember that all action can be seen as a kind of 'potential story', meaning a kind of elementary induction of the narrative." (2000: 28)

and which Romano offers to translate by the word *montrance*. The incident occurs to the *advenant* and radiates around itself, radiates in its context. In a text, in an artwork, that radiance echoes in the situations, characters, discourse of the narrator, inscribing them in a dynamics proper to narrativity.

It seems necessary here to put forward a precision on the notion of event, on its comprehension. In reality, that conception of the event seems to have to be distinguished from its formalist and structuralist acceptation, in so far as the event does not have to be accounted for, to be enumerated. The event on which narrativity is based doesn't refer to unities one can identify; narrativity is determined by the fact that *il y a événement (an event arises).* "It happens", one would say, to show the non-quantifiable character of the event, rather than its occurrences, when it's in keeping with a structuralist way of thinking. Obviously, that conception does not lead to the forming of a parameter of operative analysis, allowing to determine the *x* or *y* textual moment when it all topples over, when the text itself becomes narrative. It is more in the perspective of a phenomenology that the event makes sense and that it makes possible for the work to generate a feeling of narrativity.

In order to specify how that eventness can be at the source of a work, and according to which modalities, I will finally propose three types of manifestation of the event, three approaches to the *montrance* of the event. Those possibilities of presence are distinguished by the degree of proximity of the event in relation to the referent of the work or, to present it differently, by its relative distance in relation to the object of representation. The first type could be an inworld event.[17] It is the most widespread manifestation of the event in a work, based on a proximal relation to the object of representation. Narrativity is thus inscribed in the text from an event which happens to one of the subjects—and which inscribes it in a narrativity which can develop into a narrative, according to the configuration of that text. In that way, the event can correspond to an action, a combination of actions. In *Dare mo shiranai*, the event is rather a non-action: the waiting for the mother's return is a passiveness, occupied by activities of substitution, ersatz of actions (in regard to the waiting). What emerges for the children is the monotony of daily life, and the absence of the resolution of the problem created by the mother's departure. The event acts this way as a caution to the fiction; it gives the fiction its *raison d'être*[18]. Its montrance is diluted in the succession of days, at the risk of exhausting itself—or

[17] I am quite close here to the words used by Romano, *événement intramondain,* which refers to the world in which the event happens. It has the valuable advantage to neutralize the fictional or referential parameter of a narrative.

[18] For a preliminary view of the dynamics between narrative and fiction in contemporary works, see Audet (2006).

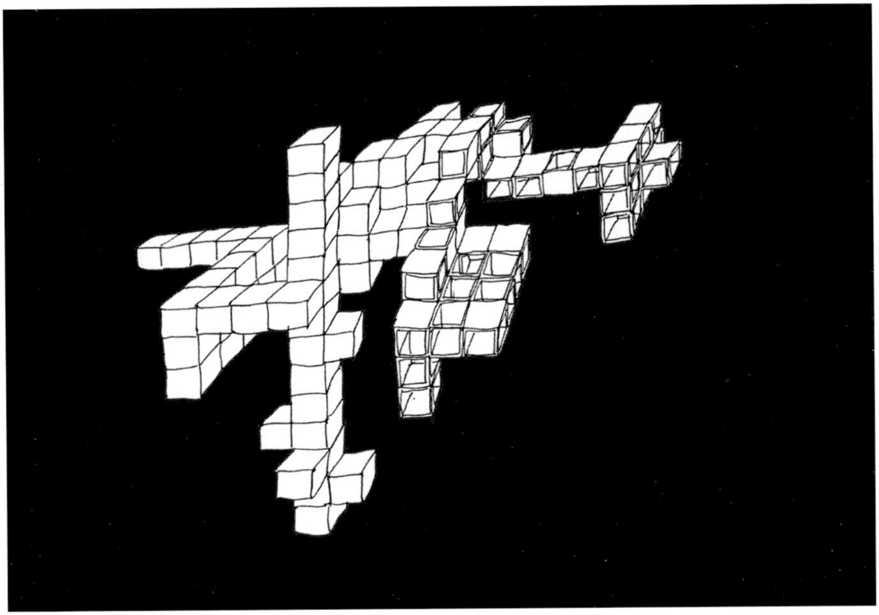

Cell City, Pia Rönicke, 2003, 4'30, vidéo still - Courtesy GB Agency, Paris et Andersen's, Copenhagen.

exhausting the narrative potential it generates at the beginning. The situation leads to the setting up of a narrativity (indeed a narrative) of substitution, formed by daily anecdotes, sporadic meetings and Yuki's death. The event is thus recipient of the fiction proposed by the film, inscribed in the heart of the world represented.

The event that induces the narrativity doesn't necessarily have to correspond to a concrete action of a character; it can be observed at the level of the discourse. The discursive event leans on linguistic data to generate a feeling of narrativity. The flow of thoughts of a character, for example, can take up a narrative shape, without for that matter being written in the diegesis, in the actions structuring a novel. Through metanarrative reflections, the discourse of the narrator of a text is sometimes constructed as to organize the narrative thread of a novel: that is precisely how Eric Chevillard's *Valiant Little Tailor* functions. In his meanders and digressions (Fludernik-like *experientiality*), the commentary of the writer-narrator constitutes the event on which the narrative discourse is based—while the Brothers Grimm tale, in that context re-written episode by episode, only figures as a lure, a statement of second importance destined to monopolize the attention of the reader. There is an event in which the writer-character, a blurred copy of the writer that emerges here and there through metafictional reflections, starts to speak. Acting in this case as caution to the discourse, the event takes charge of the statement and ascribes a narrative scope to it through the exploitation of the story potential of that discursive appearance.

The third and last type of event, in distant relation to the object of representation, is rather connected to the performing of the work itself. That operal event is a product, a result of the apparatus (textual, visual, perceptual). The existence of the work induces the reader, the spectator to perceive it in the gesture that has created it. Emerging from nothing, it results from a *man-oeuvre* that explains its presence. It is the way one perceives Lynne Cohen's photos at the moment in which they are born, the result of a grasp, a look, an event assigned to the photographer, whose look clearly shows through the choice of angles, the posture, the representation (black and white or colors).[19] The singularity of the look shows the double assignation of the event: the photographer as the *advenant* who seizes that orientated perception of the place in its potential for a story, with its "hidden stories" but also the spectator who records that disruption, who integrates it in his reading of Cohen's works and experiences the feeling of narrativity generated by the virtuality inherent in the

[19] Lynne Cohen speaks about her works as "installations", trying to convey the quality of "found objects" of the places photographed (2002: 24), as her work can be called "performance" because of the conditions to gather to succeed in catching such an image of the place (25).

image. Generally, the reader certainly perceives that operal event, but the work doesn't necessarily represent it as such. It happens nevertheless that through echoes, through a reflexivity inherent to the text, to the work, that appearance is evoked and builds, in a dual way, a structuring narrativity for that text or that work.[20] Return to the eventness producing the work on the movement that animates it: the operal event generates a two level narrativity, from which seems to emerge a double accession of the meaning to the narrative regime.

* * *

One understands that narrativity, conceived from that fundamental parameter of the event, is strongly distinguished from any definition of narrative. What happens in the narrative, that action which facilitates the occurrence of a transformation, is thus a strong inscription in the represented world of a gesture, a shattering fact; the tight weaving in which actions overlap, that plot, that teleological force results from an advanced concretization of the narrative potentiality of the event which remains, in its manifestation, short of that actantial and discursive construction. So it is rather around the three last components of the narrative that a parallel can be drawn with the narrativity as I specify it here: the maintenance of the fundamental variable of time, where the tension between a before and an after seems to generate a virtuality, that of a story to come; the assignation of the event to an *advenant* (the one which is open to an advent) imposes the presence, implicit or explicit, of a subject and, consequently, a point of view—that of the protagonist, that of the creator which strongly models the proposed representation (through a game of focalization, through the trace of perception). Such a common basis between narrativity and narrative truly confirms the conception of the narrative first offered, that of a concretisation, a complex textual and linguistic incarnation of the phenomenon of narrativity. That way we can escape the aporias of a critique coming to grips with an obliteration of the narrative, with a modulation of the narrative, a critique which is set on describing it, despite the inadequation of that notion, to understand the dynamics in place in a work.

At the end of my journey I come back to that aporia which underlies the whole textuality of Michael Joyce's hyperfiction, *Afternoon*—ironically called by its author a *story*. The reader, sent on a wrong track, (or a twisted track), tries

[20] It is the case, among other things, of poetry and its compiling, whose gesture of collecting serializes the event which constitutes the linguistic appearance of the poem; the narrativity proper to the poems collection would thus be explained by that opera.

to establish, along its navigation, the generically agreed references of the action, of the teleology, but his efforts fail each time. After this reflection, the reason seems rather obvious: the main event of that fiction is truly the emergence of the doubt. Through his refusal to dispel that doubt, through his refusal to confront the hidden story, the protagonist blocks the creation of the narrative, which would have revealed the circumstances of the accident which has probably led to his son's death.

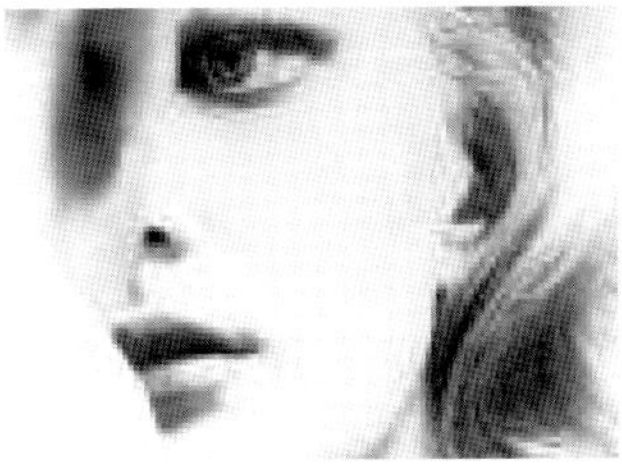

Faces, John Cassavetes, 1968 (Gena Rowlands).

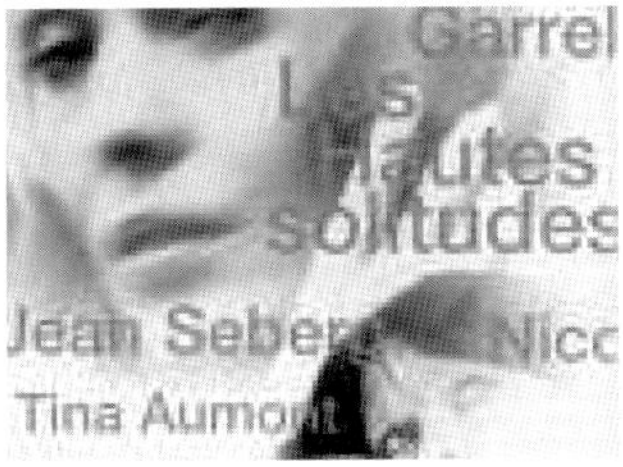

Les Hautes solitudes, Philippe Garrel, 1974 (poster detail).

TIME WORK

Seeing the way narrative actively participates in contemporary works of art, both in their construction and as the object of a reflection seeking through the narrative to re-invent other experiences of time—counter to time standardized by the formats used in the mass media—in that context, how does one tackle the question of narration today?

It should perhaps be approached in a slightly different way from that proposed by the main models of analysis available. The dominant model, until recent times, was the one put forward by structuralism, whose characteristic was to consider the text (when it is a textual narrative) in a purely immanent way, without confronting it with anything "outside", since, according to Barthes, literature doesn't refer to anything but itself, possesses a "fatally unrealistic nature". What comes from it, is that it seems superfluous, not to say incorrect, to consider the relationships that time signified by the narrative—if there is a time signified by the narrative, which I believe there is—maintains with the time of our experience. Under what the structuralists have called the referential illusion, even realism doesn't refer to anything, it's nothing more than a new code. It doesn't denote reality, it connotes it, producing an "effect of reality" which is reduced to a textual effect. At the same time, what corresponds to the referential illusion, on the narrative level, is the "chronological illusion": there is no such thing as the time of the narrative, or time in the narrative—except for the time of reading. According to that model, structural analysis of narration should put forward large "functions", "roles" (*actants*), etc., without ever questioning the way the narrative works at a much simpler and daily level, for example, when we recount episodes of our life or somebody else's life. What happens in a narration, Barthes says, is literally nothing. It is language and nothing else, "the adventure of language whose advent never ceases to be celebrated". In relation to that type of approach, it seems to me that one should try to restore organic links which bind the literary narrative, for example, to the narrative in the context of ordinary lives, and the links of the latter with our experiencing of things. That was already in some way what Aristotle undertook, but it can be developed in a different way, for example, with the tools of phenomenology.

To my knowledge, that kind of work remains to be done. One could question, for example, one of the important means of narration: the play on the differences which exist between the three levels of every narrative, literary, cinematic or other: the level of the characters who appear in the narrative, the level of the person who enunciates the narrative (or the level which films that narrative) and finally the level of the reader or the spectator. In a literary or historical narration, there is inevitably a difference between the narrative level and the time of the characters who live the story, who are immersed in it. The narrator is the one who knows what's going to happen, something the characters are obviously ignorant about. As for the reader, he is in an intermediary situation which is neither of those two situations, since he is not the one who lives the action in the present, nor the one who knows the entirety of the story. He operates, let's say, a constant coming-and-going between the two.

What represents, from a linguistic point of view, the complex play between those three levels, is what Arthur Danto calls narrative predicates. They are predicates that refer to the future and can only be enunciated by virtue of some knowledge possessed by the narrator of what's going to happen in the story as it unfolds. For example, if I say that, "*Impression, Sun Rising* is the birth of Impressionism", I give that painting a property which it only possesses if one knows the subsequent history of the movement to which it has given birth. Such predicates, which can only be enunciated retrospectively by virtue of a knowledge of what follows, only appear in a narration. From that point of view, one can contrast narration to historical accounts. In historical accounts, events follow one another in the present, each is reported for itself. On the opposite, as soon as one enters the dimension of the "diegesis", meaning the actual narration, one considers that story from the point of view of its outcome, the evidence of which is shown by the apparition of those "narrative predicates". One of the main problems is then to understand what are the (possible and real) relationships between the narrative voice which knows the outcome of the narrative, the characters who live the story in the present, and a reader (or a spectator) who also discovers the story and possesses a kind of ubiquity between those two points of view. It would be interesting to think about what corresponds to that situation in cinema: it is clear that the editing, with its ellipses, its flash backs, its flash forwards, etc, tears the cinematic narration away from the simple reporting order of historical events. There is a narrative chronology because the future is open, in other words because there is a play, a gap, between what the editing shows us from a structural point of view (according to which the outcome is already known), what the characters live in the present, and what the spectator progressively discovers while viewing the scenes but also in understanding and appreciating the editing. The time then becomes a dramatic time. All of that can be said from a still relatively internal point of view.

It seems to me that an additional level of analysis should still be added. It is at that level in reality that all of this really takes on a meaning—for I think it is not enough to analyze that narrative structure in an immanent way. All this takes on a meaning in relation to a temporality which is this time not that of the narrative, but that of our existences. How is it that we read a text as an *open* story, in spite of the closure of its narrative device, that we attend a film as if it was an open plot, when, at the moment of the projection, the entire construction of the film is already made? How can we, in other words, project ourselves into the story? How can we not only take an interest and pleasure in that narrative, but experience it and live it like a story? I don't think it's enough to answer by invoking the three narrative levels.One should rather question the relationships that the formal (discursive, filmic) construction has with a very different temporality: the temporality of our experience which is an *entirely open* temporality, where the future is a completely undetermined future. And because the future there is open, the present is never closed either. To "live" a narrative device as a true story, one has to bring it close to the structuralization of the stories we can actually *live*.

What characterizes the temporality of our stories? It would take some length to answer that. I simply want to indicate an aspect of that temporality by focusing my talk on the notion of event. Levinas says somewhere that the important experiences of our life have never been lived. That doesn't mean, naturally, that they are not "experiences", but rather that, where there is an experience in the strong sense of the word, where there is an event, what we experience that way only takes on its true meaning afterwards, depending on the possibilities it opens, the role it ends up playing in our existences. An event only appears as an event afterwards. It is never an event, but it *will have been* an event. Its tense is the future perfect. So there are events which can be prominent at the moment, which can be striking at the time, others which can be, on the contrary, as Nietzsche said, "carried on dove's feet", in other words, non-apparent, innocuous, at first glance insignificant; but, whatever the way they appear at the time, what will make them events is that they will appear *afterwards* as having been decisive, having opened a new story or a new chapter in our story.

This temporality is that of our experience before it can be represented by the complex mechanism of narration. I don't believe that the formal narrative mechanisms teach us anything about the time of our existence. It's the opposite, even if it is not ruled out to assume that the relationship between those two levels is more complex than that of a mere diversion. To understand the narration, one has to understand not only the differences which exist between the three formal levels which I mentioned earlier, but also those which exist between the narrative mechanism itself and the temporality of our existence, that time we could call completely open, in which no possibility for narrative overhang exists. We can tell our story afterwards, but in reality we are well aware—it is anyway what all those who practice autobiography say—that the way we will recount the episodes of our life will vary according to the evolution of that life. Thus, there are never any *definitive* memoirs. But the literary form that the memoirs take is "definitive". On the one hand, we have a temporality for which no form of overhang, synopsis, or ultimate summing up is possible; on the other, there is the temporality of the narrative that always has a *de facto* closure. Indeed all narratives need to be completed and can only be read as narratives once completed. Thus, even the most incomplete narrative is finished in principle; even the one that has the most inconclusive form has precisely that conclusion.

The problems posed by a phenomenological approach to the narrative seem to me to be situated at the crossing of the—could we say—uncontrollable character of the eventemential temporality and the always domesticated character of the narrative; even there the narrative makes use of formal strategies to show to what extent the time it is dealing with cannot be domesticated. To take an example, Faulkner, in his novels, very often thrives on showing the impossible-to-control nature of some events that are keys to the plot. Very often the narration develops like some kind of proliferation, making a thicket around a main emptiness, the emptiness of an event. "Emptiness", because, very often, the characters just can't recount it, or else they report it in a way which is contradictory, or again, as in *Absalom! Absalom!,* that event only appears through the gaps in the text itself. Just think about the main episode of the murder of Charles Bon by Henry Sutpen: it is only evoked through the slamming of a door that shuts.

It seems to me that the problems of narration can be approached—it is merely a suggestion—from the tension existing between the purely structural considerations linked to the relations between the three levels of the narrative which I have singled out and the temporality of the existence in its structuration by founder events. That implies one agrees to leave behind a purely internal analysis and confronts a textual (or cinematic) architecture with a different temporality. In that sense, I would disagree with Ricœur, whose thesis, in *Temps et récit*, is that the phenomenological structuration of time can only be described through the detour of an analysis of the configuration of time by the narrative. There is, in Ricœur, a kind of "linguistic idealism": experience would be formed through and through by the language, by the discursive, narrative mechanisms. Now I don't think one can show how these textual configurations "model" time if one cannot describe the time outside those modelizations—describe it in the special meaning of the word, that it would be necessary to specify too. Ricœur's linguistic idealism is not so far from that of structuralism, except that the latter is an absolute idealism ("there is no outside-the-text"), while Ricœur's would be rather a transcendental idealism: time is shaped through the categories of the narrative.

Should one distinguish between narration and narrativity? Doesn't narrativity generate another temporality?

There is a very important aspect I haven't spoken about yet, because I've only spoken until now about time shaped by narratives, and time outside the narrative. It is, let's say, the time of the encounter with the work. That time is still another time, if I may say, is another stratum of time… I do not think the work of art fits into the time of existence. It doesn't either merely enclose the time in itself, or signify it through narrative mechanisms. There is a time of encounter with the work that is a suspended time. I can't find any other word than that one, as insufficient as it is. It is not on the side of time or outside time… The encounter with the work happens in a present, which resembles that of playing, celebrations, or ritual. What characterizes them? Let's take playing, for example. In a way, there is neither beginning nor end. Obviously, the activity of playing begins and ends, but it doesn't take place, contrary to other activities, in the limits ascribable to its objective duration. One starts playing by entering a limitless time, where the play can—rightly—last indefinitely, where it has never started, but re-starts continually. One enters the time for playing, its suspended time, by suspending one's daily occupations, one's activities geared towards a purpose. To be able to enter the time for playing, one has to be able to lose oneself in it, in a way. One is in it only when one is completely immersed in it. The one who plays immerses himself in the playing, he is caught by the playing, caught in the playing, taken by the playing. Look at a child playing: he has perhaps started playing at a certain moment, but he prolongs and carries on his old games; he will undoubtedly stop at a certain moment, but the moment when he stops is dictated by something else, the game itself could carry on indefinitely. As soon as one is playing, one goes on and on playing. That is the reason why that time resembles celebration times, which are a kind of parenthesis in the midst of our working life, our tasks and daily routines. The same could be said about the time of the ritual, for example, the tea ceremony in Japan. The question is not about knowing what is its objective duration, it is about being entirely in the time in which it lasts.

The encounter with a work of art, if it is a true encounter, if something existential occurs in it—and I believe that in every artistic encounter something existential occurs—is also an event in our existence: the first time one reads Proust, Kafka, or sees an Antonioni film. As an event, it is dependent on the historical temporality of our existence. But, if one strives to describe more precisely the modalities of that encounter, one has to say that it happens in a suspended time, in a time when, through that suspense itself, the work takes on a particular presence. There is in the mode of presence to the work something that reminds us of the definition that Aristotle gives of living. Life only exists in acts, Aristotle says, a potential life is a contradiction. From the moment an organism possesses life, it possesses it in act, *en energia*. What characterizes the *energia*, or a very close notion, the *entelecheia*, is that it always possesses in itself its own term, its own end: *en telos echein*, meaning life doesn't lack anything, and nothing can complete it any further. In the same way, what characterizes the works of art, including, I believe, very contemporary works which refuse to submit to categories like that of "beauty", is a certain mode of presence where nothing can be added to the piece, to its influence and the intensity of that presence, without destroying it.

Does that mode of presence induce the possibility of the spectator taking part?

Exactly. It generates a participation that one can try to specify by completing somehow the analysis of the playing. I think about two analyses: Winnicott's and Gadamer's, which, besides, connect on numerous points.

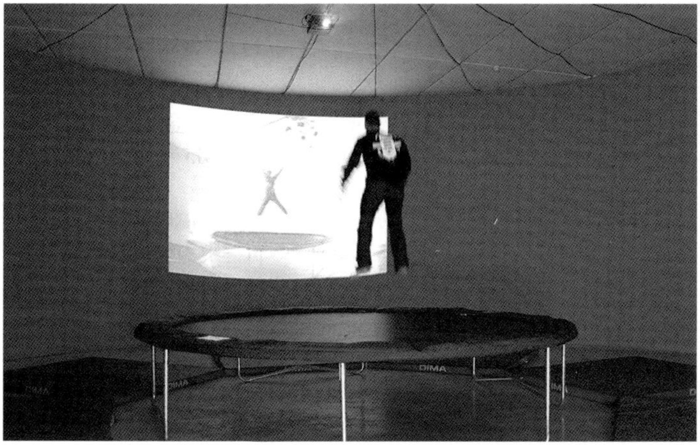

Derrière le monde flottant de Mathieu Briand (SYS*016.JeX*02/SE-FX\ 360) - visitor on the trampoline - Musée d'Art Contemporain - Lyon, 2004.

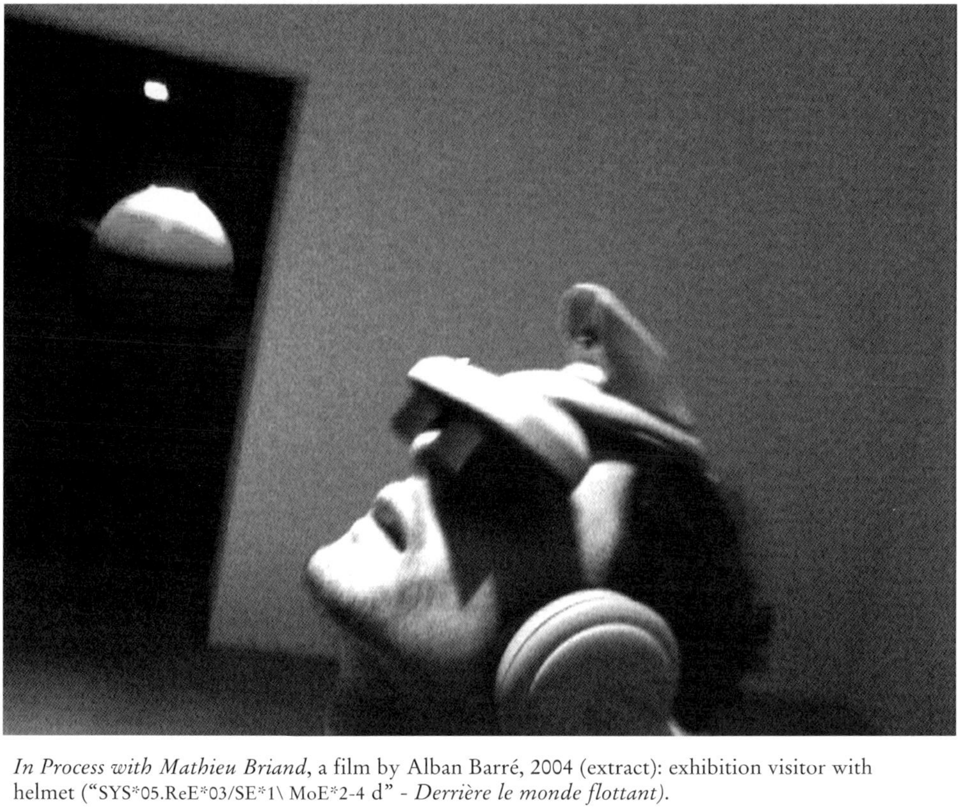

In Process with Mathieu Briand, a film by Alban Barré, 2004 (extract): exhibition visitor with helmet ("SYS*05.ReE*03/SE*1\ MoE*2-4 d" - *Derrière le monde flottant).*

Winnicott, when he talks about the child at play, creates the notion of "transitional space". His model is the playmate, the favorite teddy, the soft toy of the child. What is it about that toy? Where is it situated? Winnicot says that it is neither something which would be dependent strictly speaking on the reality, nor something which would be dependent on the subjective sphere, a representation or a phantasm; it is something situated between the two, in a neutral space, a space between the subject and the object. That sort of toy, the "transitional object" as Winnicot calls it, is at the same time the support for imaginary projections, a concrete continuation of that imaginary in the world, and of what, being already outside the child, allows him or her to gradually learn to domesticate that exteriority with all that is threatening and frightening about it. Winnicott adds that the artist is in a similar relationship *vis-à-vis* his work of art. There is a play which builds up between the work and the artist, and that work is neither subjective nor objective, it unfolds its presence in a transitional space; the artist is thus in a relationship to the work that is never pure exteriority. His work is for him a way to control the pure adversity of the world, its fundamental strangeness and misery. And, at the same time, he never really controls that work completely; it also escapes him through one side or the other. It is in that place that the imaginary can be born. For the artist, his work is like a playmate, and to see it like that, to see it like a work of art, it's necessary to enter with it in that quasi-ludic relationship where its virtualities and its powers, that the artist prolongs, and accomplishes, manifest themselves. In the same way, the person who looks at a painting must enter into some kind of playful participation with what he's looking at: the canvas is teeming with itineraries for the eyes, with possibilities which possess at the same time a free and regulated, a fortuitous and prescribed nature. The eyes meander in it. Like the act of playing, art establishes an always complex and original relationship between rule and chance.

The other analysis I'm thinking of and which, I believe, goes entirely in the same direction, is Gadamer's. There are many philosophers who have reflected on the act of playing, and there are two main ways, it seems to me, to tackle that question: either one insists on the absence of external finality of ludic activities, or one insists on the rules which underlie them. The first definition would be "Pascalian" even though Pascal insists on saying that ludic activities (hunting, where one hunts, not for the catch, but for the hunt itself) are never *completely* devoid of external purposes: they are often diversions from boredom too. But the problem doesn't lie there. According to that definition, playing is an autotelic activity, one could say, which has its limit within itself. The second perspective, which puts forward the notion of rule, is, for example, that of Wittgenstein. Obviously, there are games for which the rules are vague: tennis, for example, doesn't stipulate at which height the ball must pass over the net.

What's interesting in Gadamer's approach is that he starts from a much vaster notion of play that can apply, for example, to the play of waves. Why does one talk about "the play of waves"? Undoubtedly because, when one watches the waves, one cannot not be taken by their movement, one cannot not participate in it, one cannot not be drawn like one is by music (and, besides, don't we also talk about the violinist "playing"?). One cannot observe the waves as simple objects; one is captured, captivated, by their movement. One is caught in their "play". The swirl of the waves, their undertow is hypnotic. And the important notion, here, is that of being "caught in the game". In the game we are caught by the game. That idea is present in an etymology, undoubtedly fantasist, of the word "illusion": *illusio* would presumably come from *ludeo*, to play, hence to be caught or taken by the game. One cannot play without being literally in the illusion, taken by the game and, from the moment one is taken by the game, the remarkable fact is that the one who plays is also played, in a way, by that with what he is playing, meaning he is no longer in a relation of exteriority with that thing, nor does he control it completely. It is then understandable that games, as different as they can be, have nonetheless something in common or, at least, strong resemblances. For example, a game as simple (and devoid of rules) as to stack up pebbles or to play with sand... We are no longer dealing with simple objects... The sand, the pebbles acquire a life... we are lost in them...

And thus, we are taken by the game. The one who plays with something doesn't only carry on that thing, a teleological activity, but the activity he practices reflects in a way on him, in so far as he renounces controlling entirely that with which he is playing; if the control was total, he would stop playing altogether, he would stop being in the game. We are very close to what Winnicott was talking about, as well as to the suspended time I was mentioning earlier, a time that can expend indefinitely. The time in which the child at play is immersed, for example, is no longer the time of his own story, of the individual existence, it is the time of an encounter continually re-played with what is neither entirely his own, nor entirely other.

The notion of play is very present in contemporary art, in cinema with devices that involve the spectator. But, in order to play, one has to be able to participate, thus, to enter that work of art. How does one enter a work of art?

I think that notion of play employed to describe art is something rather old—Kant is perhaps the first to have put that in place, or at least to have suggested that, when he talks about the "free play of faculties", followed by Schiller, but one could go back further than that. Aristotle already quoted a phrase by Agathon: "Art likes chance and chance likes art." And Aristotle insists rightly on the fact that every artwork unfolds in the space between the *phusis* and the *tukhè*, nature and chance. Consequently, the artist, contrary to the craftsman, never completely controls what he's going to produce; he lets nature act outside and inside him. But, undoubtedly, it is the "aesthetics of the spirit" which has given that question on play a really central position. Because the idea of the aesthetics of the spirit is that, contrary to the normative aesthetics which imply that there are rules which allow us to pass judgements on art, to appraise the beauty or perfection of a work of art, which allow us to be a "connoisseur" in the art field, therefore which makes of art an object of knowledge (think about the golden number or the three unities in tragedy)—the idea of the aesthetics of the spirit is to say that the artist doesn't have to follow any rules, nor to copy models that he would borrow from the history of art. We could almost say that the artist receives his rules directly from "nature", he creates in a quasi-unconscious way, or, which is almost the same, he works out his own rules while creating. In Kant, it leads, for example—because the aesthetics of the "spirit" has a considerable influence on the way Kant reflects on things—to say of beauty that it is an "endless finality", a definition that could be applied exactly to a ludic activity. It is in the filiation of the aesthetics of the spirit that Kant declares there is no "determining" rules in the aesthetic judgement which would allow us to positively establish what is beautiful and what is not, but there is only place here for a "reflecting" judgement, submitted to the sole legislation of the "free play of faculties".

Therefore, it seems to me that even very contemporary art hasn't completely broken free from that tradition, and remains dependent upon it... Like the aesthetics of the spirit, it refuses all idea of normativity of aesthetic judgement—even though, obviously, many contemporary artists would refuse to refer to the "spirit"... Each work of art is a space where rules appear which are the rules fitted to the encounter with *that* work of art. The work of art must, in a way, "stage" the principles that allow us to approach it in its singularity. And to that is added, indeed, what you talk about, the fact that the distinction between the work and the spectator tends to be criticized, contested, questioned. In a certain number of installations, the spectator is invited into the work; he almost becomes an integral part of it.

You talk about art as object of knowledge. But for the spectator invited into the work, and who isn't necessarily a "connoisseur", that knowledge, establishing a critical distance with the work, passes for a sensitive experience which will modify his vision on things...

That art is an instrument of knowledge seems to me a truth deserving to be re-conquered. But I don't mean it at all in the sense of a normative conception of art! It is not art that obeys a knowledge of preliminary, immutable rules; it's rather art that is a means of knowledge. That idea is to be re-conquered, for it has been damaged by the birth of the eighteenth century's "aesthetics". The horizon of aesthetics, in the sense it has with Baumgarten, is still that which circumscribes a good deal of contemporary approaches to art. What we need to question again is the dichotomy that has appeared with modern aesthetics between art and truth. Of course, Baumgarten still speaks of "aesthetic truths" that he places next to "logical truths". Those are dependent on true knowledge, the knowledge of the universal; the aesthetic truths are in the category of minor knowledge, of a *cognito inferior*, for they don't rise to the universal. Baumgarten doesn't decline from talking about "knowledge" in art, but he thinks that that knowledge is of a purely emotional sensitive nature. After him, it is the very idea of knowledge in art and through art that will tend to disappear.

But why would the work of art be offered solely to the senses? Obviously there is a perceptive appearing of the work that is consubstantial to it. But in that encounter, another thing is played which is not of the category of the perceptive, nor even in relation to the imagination. The work is a means of comprehension, what makes the irreplaceable nature of art in the field of thought. Because art thinks, it develops, as Merleau-Ponty says, not so much ideas than the "matrix of ideas", thus, ideas on an infra-conceptual level which, however, remain for "thought" a permanent resource.

Undoubtedly, contemporary art disturbs or shifts those divisions that are those of "aesthetics" and on which art has lived in the eighteenth and nineteenth centuries. There are several ways to do that. What makes the singularity of a work of art in that optic is precisely that it makes us think, but in a form which is indissociable from the meaning of what it communicates to us. The form of a novel is totally part of its content and that's the reason why the notion of "form", favored by structuralism, remains insufficient. The form is not a code which would be the analogon of that which rules our linguistic productions. In art, form is not a formula, even a mathematical one. As soon as it becomes a formula, it ceases to offer itself as a form.

One can contrast that with practices in contemporary art, like conceptual art, in which one sometimes wonders to what extent the form I'm talking about has disappeared, to what extent the ideas have not purely and simply supplanted Merleau Ponty's "matrix of ideas". The support itself becomes almost anecdotal. With such art works, if they are still to be considered art works, we touch the question of the limit of art. It seems to me that conceptual art perhaps has a critical function, but it doesn't have a true artistic perenniality. It quite precisely corresponds, in my eyes, to what Hegel meant by his formula about "the end of art". That formula doesn't mean that art would be finished, in the sense that there would no longer be any art or artists. To understand what Hegel means, we have to understand first how he opposes the whole tradition of modern aesthetics, whose leading term he nevertheless takes on board, that of "aesthetics". Hegel thinks that art is linked to truth. Beauty, for example, he says, is "the tangible manifestation of the idea": there is a content of truth in art that art expresses with its own resources, in other words, through its tangible immediacy. At the same time, for Hegel, that truth in art is only fully reached when one goes beyond its tangible immediacy, meaning in its conceptual clarification. The artwork remains thus "inadequate to the concept", even though it is its prefiguration, and philosophy finds itself invested with the privilege of manifesting the content of art in a more adequate way than art itself, in emancipating that content of tangible forms in which it remained a prisoner. Art has to have an "end", less in the sense of a term than of an accomplishment, thanks to a *Aufhebung*, a philosophical substitution. In a way, conceptual art is the exact staging of the death of art according to Hegel. It corresponds to the idea that the work of art itself can hide behind a conceptual content which can be expressed independently from it, and which, if pushed, could be free—ideally—of all inscription in a form.

That newly acquired freedom with regard to an inscription in a form perhaps has hastened the disappearance of the object in art. Today we no longer create objects, but processes for sharing, for exchanges, for common experimentations. Even though there are objects, the object is no longer the finality.

That's right, the object is no longer the finality, but the thought behind it is. We still need to know if it is a disappearance of the object in art or a disappearance of art in the object...

What I mean is that we must distinguish between works where that thought and creative procedure which are those of the artist remain in spite of everything linked to the work, which in itself can be a process, a journey, whose technical aspect can even be an important component, but where, however, the ideal or cognitive content remains linked to the form, even if that form has exploded, demultiplied, or is infinitely reproducible, etc… and works as found in conceptual art, where, if pushed, the form doesn't generate a thought process. It has become a pretext. And there where it becomes a pretext, the question of the end of art is definitely put across. It is about an end that is not simply the "end" in the banal sense of the term, but the perspective according to which art could be taken over by an *Aufhebung* of a different order. What is striking in the new arts is that the support tends to get reduced, to be abstracted, and to vanish into thin air. The work of art can become intangible and be reduced to a device. Cinema first required film stock, a screen, and a projector; today, with digital, that device becomes much more volatile. The support is no longer part of the work. It is however necessary to distinguish between that abstraction of the support and the creation of new forms being in league with time. In some arts, the work no longer is a *monumentum aere perennius*, a thing whose vocation is to remain and last forever, and it is no longer something where the dimension of the completion takes on a decisive character. It becomes close to a Heraclitean flux... but a form remains, despite everything. The volatilization of the support is not the volatilization of the work of art.

Even the most ephemeral works, the most transitory prepare their space for presence, and thus, for encounter. The painting remains unchanged and we have to linger next to it, to start to clear a path to it, to start to really see it. It's very different with cinema or music. One of the questions specifically posed by Benjamin concerns the technical reproducibility of works of art, and how it deeply modifies the way we experience them. Doesn't the fact that we can purchase in CD form any great interpretation of a concerto and listen to it at home modify the way our relation to music unfolds? I think the answer is yes. To go to a concert has a ceremonial aspect: one has to first wait, to keep quiet; music is only played once, we have to be entirely available for the time it lasts. We experience the interpretation as a unique event, a non-repeatable event. We listen to our CDs much more distractedly, for we are under the illusion that we can always listen to them again and again. I'm talking about illusion, for we miss that way (and in a sense forever), the moment of encounter, which is unique, singular. Benjamin has a word to designate the mode of presence to a work of art which provides the dimension for a possible encounter, and that's the word "aura". Technical reproducibility tends to strip the work of the "aura" which surrounded it, and gave it its inimitable presence. Even what can be reproduced—and the work of art has always been to some extent reproducible, a painting could be copied, etc...—possesses that quality of presence that no copy can reproduce: that is what is modified with many contemporary art pieces, which no longer are dependent upon a material support...

...and which are sometimes events...

Some can be happenings, others, performances, others still only dependent on technical devices for their diffusion. With the Internet, one can acquire films at home like one acquires running water or electricity by turning on the tap; with the press of a button, images reach us, a flux of images... I think that one of the main problematics of cinema, since the sixties at least, is the resistance that the cinematic artwork offers to its technical reproducibility, to its technical part.

In what way has our experience of art changed with that evolution of technology and media?

I was talking about "aura" as Benjamin meant it: a presence of the art work in that suspended time which is that of our encounter with it and of which Benjamin seemed to say in his text on "The work of art in the era of mechanical reproduction", that the cinema obliterated it almost entirely. He said, in quite a strange way, that the attention we give to a film is an "inattentive" attention. He was comparing that type of attention with that we give to what was called in his time the *mass media*, especially the information transmitted by the radio and, later, television.

I don't think Benjamin is right on this point. In his analysis of the information in the age of the media, there is that idea that far from making the events reported to us in dramatic fashion, closer, more experimental, more comprehensible, the media tends to inflict mini-traumatisms on us which—as is the attribute of any traumatism—remain impossible for our experience to assimilate. Rather, the effect of those pseudo-traumatisms makes us more distant from the information we receive. That seems right and profound to me. Since, one has often insisted on the ambiguities of compassion from afar, on their perverse effects. But Benjamin compared cinema a little too hastily to mass media and propaganda. There is not that loss of critical conscience in cinema that the media often provoke. The way cinema has developed, shows it. While remaining under the constant threat of a system of "production" and "exploitation" (the words are important) which subjects it to technical and commercial constraints, while remaining an art submitted, more than any other, undoubtedly, to those constraints, cinema, or a certain cinema, continues to authentically be concerned with art. The situation is thus complex. It would be wrong to say that technology by itself, or the laws of the market by themselves (two separate but connected constraints), are by nature responsible for causing the "loss of aura" mentioned by Benjamin. On the contrary, cinema is perhaps first defined *against* the consumable, the disposable images, the images-waste produced by television—those that Woody Allen refers to in *Annie Hall* in that scene when the character played by Allen, drives, in the company of Annie Hall, through a residential district of Los Angeles, perhaps Beverly Hills or Encino, and she exclaims: "it's strange how clean it is here, compared to New York", and the character played by Allen replies, "it's normal, their trash is shown on television."

The image, at the time of Benjamin, still belonged to the artists. At the end of the twentieth century, the press and television convey it, in order to inform us. The artists, dispossessed, applied themselves to re-work the images from the media to disinform them, in a way, to give them another information, in another form of reality to experience, to experiment, to see as another reading of the world.

Yes, for example, in video art, in some installations using images, photos, films that have gone round the world, like those of the attacks of 9/11 in 2001... We could say that regarding those images, whose broadcast in a loop for hours on end tended to short-circuit, at least for a while, the ability to reflect, and to anaesthetize our critical sense to leave us only horrified and dumb-struck (a perfect example of those pseudo-traumatisms that information inflicts on us, as mentioned by Benjamin), regarding those images which have been watched so much, the artists claim a right to a certain "right of looking"... A different right of looking, a highly political right of looking, which is part of that critical dimension that art has assumed much more frequently since the eighteenth century.

Cinema and video art are in conflict with the media, as painting was in conflict with photography or cinema, and that conflict is productive in so far as it forces us to question again and again the relationships between art and non-art.

Not so long ago in the Chicago Museum I saw Hopper's *Nighthawks* again. Three solitary figures can be seen, two men and a woman, elbows leaning

Blow-up, Michelangelo Antonioni, 1966 (David Hemmings, Vanessa Redgrave).

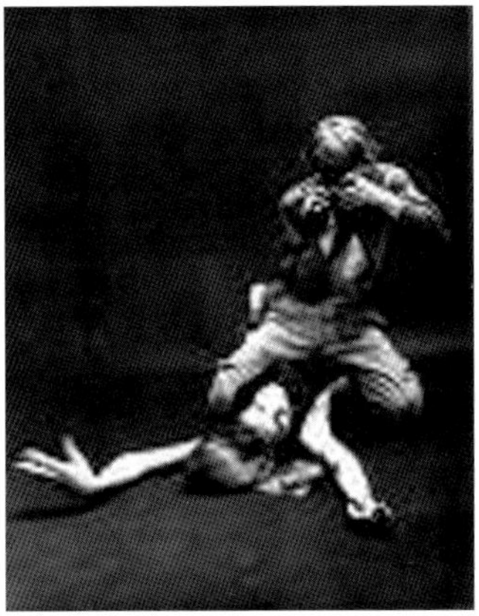

Le piège sur lui se referme
chaque seconde compte
malgré ses efforts, l'intervention de son frère, de ses proches, l'adultère sera dévoilé dans quelques jours
malgré ses efforts pour empêcher la sortie des photos du scandale, [NDLR : on sait qu'il a fait pression sur **M. S*****, le paparazzo (et ami de **Fili Houteman**) qui fut l'auteur de cette machination, organisa la rencontre dans le seul but de prendre des photos (voire de faire une vidéo) et de les revendre pour une petite fortune]

*M. S*** fabrique des événements réels*

l'intervention de son frère et de proches
0h : Ivre mort il réveille **Stéphanie** et avec des mots embrumés d'alcool il avoue, il lui explique la trahison.
Sous le choc : comment crier sa douleur et sa tristesse
elle fuit il la rattrape fou furieux, est sur le point de la maltraiter : il réclame son droit.

terrible ironie du calen-drier : il y a tout juste quatorze ans, ce samedi **14 septembre**, **Grace** disparaissait dans un tragique accident de voiture et comme si tout cela ne suffisait pas, le magazine italien **Oggi** publie une photo de **Caroline**

Grimaldi (la famille) [juste avant, **Rainier** se reposait loin de la Principauté, après une grave opération du cœur : NDLR]
fragile du cœur depuis son triple pontage coronarien
à l'héliport 17h28 sa

Laquelle est la vraie ?

surprise dans son jardin de **St Rémy** totalement chauve. Émoi en principauté.

Plusieurs hypothèses ont été émises : outre celle d'une grave maladie, on suppose que cette calvitie soudaine serait liée à des troubles d'origine psychosomatique dûs à un choc plus ou moins ancien. D'aucuns, cependant, prétendent avec optimisme que la princesse suivrait une nouvelle mode [NDLR : on aurait photographié l'actrice **Demi Moore**, le crâne entièrement rasé, elle aussi] **Caroline** est presque méconnaissable
dans son refuge de **Saint Rémy**

a démenti la rumeur : une maladie grave
Caroline a caché son crâne rasé sous une casquette le **14 septembre**
malade et encore solitaire
pour se rendre au palais
nous sommes le **14 septembre, il est 18h 30 passées à Saint Rémy** (Provence)
fini le temps où le couple descendait fièrement les marches du palais
A minuit, c'est une véritable malédiction qui frappe ce **15 SEPTEMBRE** à Monaco les

démarche est pesante, il sort

L'hologramme photographique porno sera la prochaine étape

de l'hélico on est le **jeudi 17 septembre**, il est précisément

Petits poëmes en prose, Christophe Hanna, Paris, Al Dante, 1998, p. 41.

on the counter of a bar looking out on a deserted street, and a barman, all those figures having come to a standstill, bathed in an unreal light. What struck me when I saw the painting again, is to what extent painting attempts here to reappropriate the elements typical of the cinema of the time, film noirs, B movies: same solitary figures, same gray felt hats, same inevitable scene in a bar, with that woman who could be a prostitute... the size of the painting, its framing, has something cinematic about it. It's as if the painting was saying: "this is not cinema". The intention of the artist was to take up all the motifs of the film noir to get it to say something else: we are immersed in a distended temporality, a temporality whose wait has no beginning nor end, it looks like the characters have been there forever and will be there forever. The painting reappropriates the themes of commercial cinema to pervert them and give them back a vigor, a sparkle, a glory, since that painting expresses with an incredible potency, the existential solitude of those uprooted beings that the cinema only lets us glimpse at.

To go back to the question, yes, art seems to me in permanent conflict with technology that strongly defines our contemporary world, with technology in and out of it, which becomes in itself an object of inspiration and protest and criticism through art. If there was nothing more than technology left, that would be the death of art, but art can also feed from that increasingly fragmentary, increasingly incomplete world, one could say, which is the one in which we are immersed more and more because of the devices speeding up information, communication, broadcasting of images, devices which precisely place us in a time no longer propitious to that type of encounter we were mentioning earlier, and which even contradicts it categorically. One can use the example of poetry, which always has to justify itself in the face of the tyranny of "communication" and the standardized, instrumentalized language that accompanies it.

I would like to go back on the question of the relation between art and media and that notion of loss, especially the loss of experience.

Benjamin's idea was that the media takes away our experience, and in reality only produces pseudo-traumatisms, repeated shocks which touch us all the more lightly for they strike us superficially and appear, precisely "striking". To counteract that, the artistic dimension has often manifested itself through the plenitude of the presence of the work of art, plenitude, and reality such that nothing could be added to it that would affect that plenitude. That reality is, in fact, completely the opposite of the reality of "current events", since the thing which we call the news, aspire to, and even, the "total news", as Jünger talks about "total mobilization", meaning a news which aspires to inform us totally, without respite, in real time, is precisely that quasi-simultaneity with an ensemble of things, of world events, whose absolutely contemporary objective witnesses we would be. It is a fantasy of perfect contemporaneousness with everything. To that ideology of communication in real time and total information, one could oppose Mallarmé's phrase in *Divagations*: "Badly informed is the person who would shout he is his own contemporary."

Badly informed by the news, but well and truly in-formed by it. The fantasy of that absolute contemporaneousness only conceals all the strings which contribute to give a format to the image, to force it into pre-established formats, to select it, to cut it up, to edit it, to accompany it with explanatory comments, all the complex, technical, economic, ideological devices which are those of the manufacturing of images, that the news has become.

The reality of art has nothing to do with that cult of the so-called immediacy and "real time", nor with the "direct contact" with the world that the image is supposed to give us. On the contrary, art has always claimed slowness, the fact of spending time near the art works, the absence of reality in the sense given to that word by Nietzsche, and patience. Obviously, one can have the impression that our world leaves less and less place for slowness, patience, or the reality of the non-real, therefore to that type of presence that can be that of a work of art. Is it to say, for all that, that art has changed into a product and a mere commodity? It is sometimes the way things have been understood, like, for example, in the impressive and very interesting text, though somewhat wrong in my opinion, published in *La dialectique de la raison*, and called: "The industrial production of cultural goods". In it, Horkheimer and Adorno talk about the two arts which are making the biggest impression at the time, during the emigration of the Frankfurt School to the United States: cinema and jazz. To sum it up, their thesis—which is extremely caricatural, which is even perhaps the model of what you shouldn't do in philosophy when you talk about an emerging art—consists in saying that, because cinema is a production of advanced capitalism, because it is supported by a whole complex socio-economical infrastructure and because it is an art in which the industry, the "production", specifically, plays an altogether central role, then it is no longer an art, it's merely a cultural production, a "system of non-culture", or so they say. Why? Because cinema is then a mass production, standardized, made uniform, like any other industrial production, and, in that respect, is not very different from magazines, advertising, or other forms of mass cultural production.

Horkheimer and Adorno see a confirmation of their thesis in the way scenarios are constructed in Hollywood, following an almost fixed pattern, in which the "conflict" must happen after so many minutes, the "resolution" after so many other minutes... Those codes are, they say, fundamentally commercial, thus cinema is not really an art, it's a *business*. The system presiding over the selection of actors is entirely homogeneous to society, to its expectations; even the role that chance plays in Hollywood cinema is not innocent, it is an ideological factor, that which ends up persuading the small employee or secretary, that her life could be turned on its head, from one moment to the next, while obviously, it's nothing like that at all.

That criticism of cinema's ideology as a cultural production is not wrong in itself, there are aspects of that analysis, which are entirely defensible. What it fails fundamentally to take into consideration is the role of convention in art, in every era. It is not true that convention kills art, it is one of its conditions. Think, for example, of the whole pictorial tradition in the West, up to the Baroque era. Cinema plays a comparable role, in our time, to that of painting until the eighteenth century which, for it gave access to a whole collective imaginary made of myths, stories, allegories, provided a common cultural substratum—it was called, in the Middle Ages, the "Bible for the poor" since those who couldn't read, could nevertheless follow the biblical episodes... Today, cinema has become, probably even more than the novel, our common artistic language, thus, something that is ruled by strong conventions. It is a mistake to identify the problem of convention, which is also that of a collective imaginary, with that of the standardization of cinematic creation introduced by the mass production submitted to market constraints. Those are two different problems.

Following that, Horkheimer and Adorno tend to apply their idea of an entertaining industry as a system of non-culture to the whole of the cinematic production and, in that sense, their text really seems to me a counter-example of what a philosophical analysis should be. They apply their theory with no discrimination on values; so finally, it's rather their analysis that tends to make everything uniform. They put Orson Welles on the same level as romantic comedies or B movies, saying that even when one departs from Hollywood rules, one does exactly the same, one confirms them. And one finds in their writings this extraordinary passage, in which they go as far as maintaining that the wheat fields which undulate in the wind, at the end of Chaplin's *The*

Dictator, are nothing more than a re-take of the theme of the young German camper in Nazi propaganda films!

So there is that vision of cinema as a pure "cultural production", an entertaining industry. But what I find interesting in today's cinema is the force of resistance it opposes to every process, both technical and commercial, which makes it possible—a force of resistance which in my opinion makes of cinema, at least in the twentieth century, the most central art and not because it is superior to the others, that wouldn't make any sense to suggest that, but because it is an art which truly says something about the world we're living in. It is the art that confronts the omnipotent money in our market's societies, the omnipresence of technical mechanisms, the dictatorship of the media... Cinema is the incarnation of the technology that makes it possible, the market that allows the existence and showing of films, the media which are its main support. But it is also the diversion of them.

It's the same for technology, inside and outside cinema. There is no art in which, to such an extent, the technical mechanism of the making of the film and its showing are an integral part of the work itself. Which means that there is no cinematic work of art outside the technical process that allows the making and showing of it. The history of cinema is the history of its technology, the change from silent films to speaking, from black and white to color, from the first formats to scope, and then, from super 8 to digital images. All those steps are not outside the history of cinema, but punctuate it. What seems very potent and interesting in that art, and thus, prevents us from giving an interpretation as reducing as that of the Frankfurt School, is that one of its main problematics is precisely the problematic of the cinematic artwork maintaining something of its presence, in other words, of its glory in the sense of its influence and therefore its nature absolutely irreducible to technical devices, its character of revelation, making all the forms of capture and ascendancy that technology exercises on the word, fail.

Think about Antonioni's *Blow Up*, a particularly opaque work, whose opacity is an essential feature, as always in Antonioni's films, where there are symbols but never any transparent allegories. In that film, Antonioni questions at length the future of cinema... There is that fashion photographer, if you remember. The instrumental relationship he maintains with his models is emphasized in the film. There is something predatory in photography, especially fashion photography, which compares the act of shooting to a type of sexual act (something that is amply underlined through several scenes) and, if pushed, to a symbolic murder. The whole film revolves around that issue. Photography is a technical process to capture reality, to possess it. The photographer is depicted as greedy, unscrupulous, and totally egocentric: but all of this is not to be taken in a psychological sense. There is a scene towards the end when he finds himself by chance in the middle of a rock concert. At some point, the guitar player breaks his guitar, and hurls a bit into the audience. The photographer literary tears it away and runs with it, only to abandon it a few minutes later on the pavement. In another scene, driving his Rolls Royce, he comes across a peace protest—a girl puts a placard in the back of the coupé and it falls out at the next turning… The thing at stake in the film appears to be the status of cinema, its undecidable situation, halfway between fashion photography and painting. There is, indeed, that painter friend who lives next door… In a rather fleeting scene, they talk about his latest painting. The photographer wants to buy it from him. The painter says, I resume here: "I don't know how a painting is done, there, for example, there is a leg appearing, but I never know in advance what's going to happen." When the photographer starts to shoot a couple in a park and, developing the photo, he progressively discovers a murder within the image, there is a scene when the painter's girlfriend comes to see him and says that the blow-up photos in which the grain brings to mind brushstrokes, makes her think of her partner's paintings… Cinema wavers between those two tendencies, that of a technical device, rather factitious and, in the end, non-artistic—that fashion photographer is the opposite of an artist—and that of an equivalent to painting, for photography appears, in the course of the film, like the place of truth, and even, of revelations, since those photos, taken at the beginning, with no other intention than to steal something from the couple's intimacy, finally let the truth of the crime which has happened appear, and that the photographer hasn't seen first, wholly absorbed as he was in his "shooting". For one never sees what one shoots at the moment one shoots it, I mean one always photographs what one did not see. There is something here which inexorably escapes, the body of reality, the body of the crime in a way, that corpse which has finally disappeared, at the end of the film, when the photographer comes back for the last time to the spot where he had discovered it. Therefore, there is something that escapes, even there, where the most perfected technical device to capture reality entirely is at work. And it is because something escapes that there is still room for art, in spite of the technical, economic, commercial constraints. That body of reality which has disappeared is the one evoked by that very beautiful end in which the photographer finds himself near a tennis court, where young people wearing theatre make-up mime a tennis match without a ball. The ball has disappeared, like the corpse. The technical device could not completely encompass it, capture it. Cinema thus remains like that, suspended, like the film it is that place of disclosure where truth always evades us, despite being caught by the look, despite the technical devices. Is cinema, fashion photography, anti-artistic and commercial, or is it painting? That is exactly the question posed by the film, an anxious question with no reply.

Therefore there is that side through which one could say that cinema has achieved after all the old western fantasy of a perfect *mimesis*, a *mimesis* so complete that it made reality pass entirely into the image. And at the same time something happens in a film when that device of technical capture encounters an adversity, an otherness such that the device itself ends up being transcended. Cinema is that life and death struggle of a technical device against itself, to allow for something to exist in the image, to precisely allow the images not to be just images. "Pas d'images justes, juste des images" (There's no such thing as a just image—there is just an image): Godard's phrase should be turned upside down too, for cinema is not just images, it's the right images, in the end. And the right images means images which truly leave room for otherness.

What sort of otherness?

That otherness is obviously multiple, it cannot be locked in a general scheme, but amongst the sharpest forms of otherness conveyed by the cinematic image, there is of course the human presence, there is the incarnated presence, not only human, but the presence of things too, but, in reality, it is a whole. That presence of bodies, that presence of faces... and that is perhaps what is the most striking, there is a way for the cinema to give life to things as to faces, to make a face of everything.

The face is the appearing of the person himself. *Persona*, the face, is also a film by Bergman (another is called *The Face*). And thus the face is that place where the other reveals himself in his offered, bare, disarmed presence. Why is the face so cinematic? Cinema, in a way, is the exchange of looks (the in- and off-camera) and the appearing of the face (the close-up). Two of its main processes are directly linked to the appearing of the face. I don't think that it has to be thought of as Levinas does at all. The face isn't something that doesn't appear, that "stands out against the phenomenality", it is exactly the opposite: it is the place of the fullest and most compact presence of someone, and therefore, something both open and transparent, transparent in its very depth. Wittgenstein wrote this: "Generally, I don't foresee the fear, I *see* it. Things don't happen as if I was inferring from an outside, the probable existence of an inside, but rather as if the human face was quasi-transparent, and that I saw it, not in a reflected light, but in its own light."

I think that it is what cinema can bring out against all the technical devices which underlie it, that possibility of making some figures appear in their own light, especially that outstanding form that is the face. You must know, by the way, that in Ancient Greek, *eidos*, the Platonic name to express the form or the idea, also has the meaning of "face". The face resists technical capture through the image. It resists with its very transparence, its opening. It resists, not through its opacity as Levinas thinks, but rather through the fact of offering itself in its own light. There is an absolutely magnificent film by Philippe Garrel, very boring but superb, *Les Hautes solitudes*. It is a decidedly amazing film for there is absolutely no plot, no *diegesis*; there are three characters—one is played by Jean Seberg that must be one of her last films—filmed in their solitude. As far as I remember, there is no dialogue. What is seen, most often in close-up, are their faces, silent. They look through the window; they light up cigarettes. We see what nobody, by definition, sees—solitude—and we see it from that place where no one can look. Those faces have at times an extraordinary incandescence, an extraordinary presence, especially Jean Seberg's. All the human emotions, all the thoughts pass across those faces, flow like the shadows of a changing sky on a landscape. To say that faces become landscapes is not at all a way to deny their humanity, on the contrary. It is through its opening to a universal intelligibility, to a universal reciprocity with every other face, that the face is what, in the image, goes beyond the resources of the image. The face reveals the truth of the image.

We find that in Antonioni's films too: he used to say, for that matter, that what he expected from his actors was not to be able to play but to be… to have the same mode of presence as that of a tree or a cloud. In Cassavettes too, *Faces* is an ode to the face, a progressive revelation of the characters through their gestures and their face, with no psychology, in which the touching side of the existential void of the characters is expressed through the carnal dimension alone of their presence. The face, and more generally the body in cinema are that presence which haunts the image and prevents it ending on a universe of images, which, besides, is a contradictory idea, for there is no universe of images, there are images which eventually open on the universe but there is no universe of images, or rather, the idea of a universe of images evokes precisely the danger of an image which would only be a device, a play of figures which would be nothing more than a formula. When Godard said that "in cinema, it's the form that thinks; in bad cinema, it's the thinking which forms," it is possible that he also alludes to the role of the body; cinema spares us the overflow of speech to let through something from reality—the idea of staging (*mise-en-scène*) is always somehow dangerous, because there is no stage (*scène*), it is something else. It's what happens outside the "scenes" which is the place where something happens in cinema.

> *Wherever it concerns cinema or the media, save what characterizes them as type of image, there is also the question of information. In both cases, there is a story we are told. For example, in the narrative research that is done in cinema today, it seems that it's precisely on that that the discussion is always turned: to counteract the narrative logic of the information carried by media (in a wide sense) images.*
> *For example, Raoul Ruiz, in his book,* Poetics of Cinema, *strives to show how the narrative paradigms of the entertainment industry or the globalization of the audiovisual world take up the narrative theories developed by Hollywood and known by the name of "the central conflict theory". It is a dualist theory inherited from the logic of Aristotle's conflict, which today dictates the way we are told stories, the way information is transmitted to us by giving us a reading of the world univocal and interchangeable.*
> *Ruiz also says that the worst thing is that even our dreams today reach us already built on that model, for the flux of images lies too on a narrative device which works our imagination thoroughly. From that stems his research on a narrative device which has to be questioned in order to apprehend the events in their multiple senses, to take back what is left on the side, like those stories whose meaning is uncertain, or which refuse the link of direct causality between a decision and the conflict which could result from it. Therefore, a research on other narrative devices introducing other modes of temporalities in order to tell stories.*

I shall answer part of the question, for it is a long one. So, the question on information. I would differentiate between Hollywood and information. Information has a form, thus it informs us in the double sense of the word. That form has a format, it complies with many requirements which have nothing to do with its actual content, with ideological, economic, commercial, political, bureaucratic requirements, and that formatting is also connected to technical constraints, for technology always goes hand in hand with the content, it is an ideological device too and nothing is more appropriate to seize or broadcast an ideology than technology. Well, that is information, that's one thing. The formatting which also exists in some Hollywood productions, at the level of the structure of scenarios, especially, is something else. Or, at least, it's partly different. There is a popular art which lies on conventions more potent than the art of the elite or intellectuals, think about Harlequin in the *Commedia dell'arte*, or Marivaux' Harlequin... Today's constraints are no "worse" than yesterday's, they are just different. But that doesn't amount to denying that they also have a commercial or an ideological aspect.

I am not convinced one should compare the "central conflict theory" to Aristotle's *Poetics* for the simple reason that what Aristotle was interested in, when he wrote the theory of tragedy, was not the idea of "conflict", but that of inversion—it is what Lallot and Dupont-Roc translate by *metabainein* and *metabasis*—from happiness to unhappiness, an inversion which was not to hit the righteous ones, nor the fundamentally bad, otherwise the tragic effect, the *catharsis*, could not happen. If one should wonder what is behind the "central conflict theory"—and I'm incapable of answering that question—I would nevertheless be inclined to say that there is the whole of the *homo economicus'* individualism, a whole "polemological" conception of society as rivalries and conflicts of interest which is proper to the modern western world—have you noticed a scenario by Ozu based on such a principle? I agree with Ruiz that the grid projected that way on reality is extraordinarily impoverishing... and also that it is wrong to believe that every scenario, in order to avoid generating boredom, should be based on that. Boredom is as cultural as everything else is.

But perhaps these new narrative devices are about questioning the link to causality?

Narration cannot totally abandon causality, for it would be abandoning narration itself. But it can question some forms of causality; those linked to the motivation for our actions, for example. Proust, Joyce or Faulkner has done little else. And cinema takes that up again. David Lynch, for example, is an expert in that field.... Do we dream following the scheme of the central conflict theory? It is tempting to think that, but I am not sure... I'd like, for that matter, to react to what you said about the image and the imagination. One could think, and it is a widely spread thesis, that images kill the imagination. In a world where the image occupies such a great place, our imagination would be impoverished. Our dreams too. I don't think it's true, for I believe that idea rests on too narrow a conception of what is the imagination.

The imagination is not only the fact of having what is called in psychology "mental images", a problematic notion, meaning to see absent things as present with the eyes of our mind, as Descartes said. The imagination can use many mediums: to invent beautiful speeches (the rhetorical art), new possibilities of action (the practical deliberation), all of that plus many other activities are also part of the imagination, without any single "mental image" being implicated. There is also a perceptive imagination one forgets too easily when one approaches those questions. That perceptive imagination is precisely that which is developed and enriched by a world placing us in the presence of more and more images. The only philosopher who ever really spoke about it is Husserl. He distinguishes between imagination, *Phantasie* in German, and the conscience of image, *Bildbewusstsein*. When you look at a photo, when you are a spectator in the cinema, you don't imagine at the same time as you perceive, in the sense that you would have some kind of "internal images" which would accompany the photograph or the film. However, your imagination is totally implicated, mobilized, but it is an imagination which entirely resides in what you perceive, which animates and vivifies the images perceived, which confers on them their density and expressive vigor. Accordingly that imagination has not at all to represent something that would be absent. There is therefore a modality of the imagination that is inside the images themselves, if one can say, in the way we can take part in the images.

As a result, one should support exactly the opposite of the thesis we were talking about: the more we see images, the more our perceptive imagination develops, refines, becomes sensitive to nuances, in the same way as the more we read, the more we are receptive to nuances of style and ways of thinking... We have here the same kind of dialectics which is that of all creation, a dialectics of learning by experience and rupture: the more cultured we are, the more we experience images, for instance, the more we learn to differentiate them, to appreciate them, to evaluate them, to classify them, and the more capable we become of creativity. I don't think our imagination is more narrow or constricted today than it was yesterday. It's the opposite.

Obviously there are restraints, conformisms that underlie the manufacturing of images. Andy Warhol based his whole work on that. It is the place of the image on the intellectual map of our culture that has changed, which no longer is peripheral, but central. For an American, cinema has become an implement to comprehend the world, a system and a grid of values, as literature or history was before. What Warhol suggests is that for the American of the Sixties, cinema is no longer understood according to reality, but reality is understood according to cinema. And that, if one wants to understand

American culture, one has to start understanding what American cinema is. But it is another question than the one we were talking about...

So when you talk about the imagination at work in cinema, could it be the link that would precisely allow investing, incarnating the image so that it recovers some materiality, contrary to the image of the media that is dematerialized?

Cinema is undoubtedly a way to "incarnate the image", to use your own words, very different, for example, from that of painting. We could infer that from the example of the treatment of the face. It is very crude to sum up things that way, but if one considers the evolution of painting in the twentieth century, especially with the Abstract movement, it is not so much a disappearance of the face one attends to, as its transformation, one could almost say its transfiguration. For example, it is very striking in the case of Malevitch: he calls his "Black Quadrilateral on White" an "icon", meaning a face, and when he conceives the coffin in which he will be buried, you know that he places that painting at the exact location of the face, of his face. The face disappears, but the painting has taken its place under the power of abstraction itself. Obviously cinema cannot produce that; it is contrary to its means. It cannot escape the order of figuration, except punctually... But the face can nevertheless take on an abstract character in the sense of non-mimetic, in cinema too. For example, in Cassavetes' films, or even in Dreyer's.

To go back on the link between the image—the imagination—the body, that imagination which invests the image in cinema by materializing it, could be in a way an image that takes shape.

I would prefer to say: an image which takes shape rather than materiality. Materiality refers more to the support... Cinema images are dense, saturated images. They are not poor images like, for example, images of video games or devices which depend on the "virtual". I'm thinking about Baudrillard's analyses, questionable but very interesting. Our world would move towards a kind of virtualization of all things and thus also of dissolution or murder of reality, which would be the "perfect crime", with no residue of a corpse. I think that there is a moment when that analysis ends suddenly because it generalizes too much, I don't think it can be applied to everything indiscriminately, from Disneyland's sugarcoated images to Warhol's paintings and the Gulf War. But what is true is that there is a kind of fantasy which is carried out in the images mastered through digital technology, that of the dissolution of the difference between reality and fabrication, the fake, the product... reality becomes a technical production. Think about those people who meet exclusively on the net and end up with no need to meet in reality. What was a means to get to know one another becomes an end in itself. All of that effectively betrays a relation to the image that becomes terribly de-realizing. I'm not talking about the image only, for one could find the equivalent in other techniques.

If we take the case of the mobile phone, for example, I have a friend, Martin Rueff, who has developed a very beautiful analysis of the fact that the mobile which, on the one hand, allows us to be permanently "close" to our nearest, on the other entirely modifies the space of interlocution. When someone phones in front of you, in a public place, for example, in a train compartment, you literally do not exist for him, as is indicated by his use of personal pronouns. Normally—imagine that you were alone with him in the compartment—"you" (*tu*) should apply to you, since "you" (*tu*) means the presence of an interlocutor, and you are the only one present. But, in this case, "you" (*tu*) is diverted from its normal function, and suddenly you become the witness, powerless, but nevertheless called to account, of a private conversation which is none of your business but which, ironically, is your business, because of the use of the personal pronoun, a use which has the result that you are at the same time invited, since present, and held as non-existent, since that pronoun which, normally, could only address you, doesn't address you at all in this case. Real relationships no longer exist, only virtual ones do (and are linguistically sanctioned). One could shift that type of analysis to other phenomenons—Heidegger underlined early on something similar concerning television, saying that television makes everything which is remote, close, but that in reality it abolishes, in a fake proximity, distance as well as proximity. No longer is there either distance or proximity; there is only a closeness that is not close.

Baudrillard generalizes that concerning what he calls "the hyper-reality". What the virtual does is to produce hyper-reality, meaning something where the distinction between real and virtual itself, between the image and what it is the image of, has disappeared. And that is—allow me to make a parenthesis again—Plato's old dream, or rather, old nightmare. What is surprising is that at the beginning of western reflection on the image itself, there is the example of Zeuxis' grapes (Zeuxis, that painter who was so skilful at painting grapes that birds were fooled and used to come and pick at the images). The image is

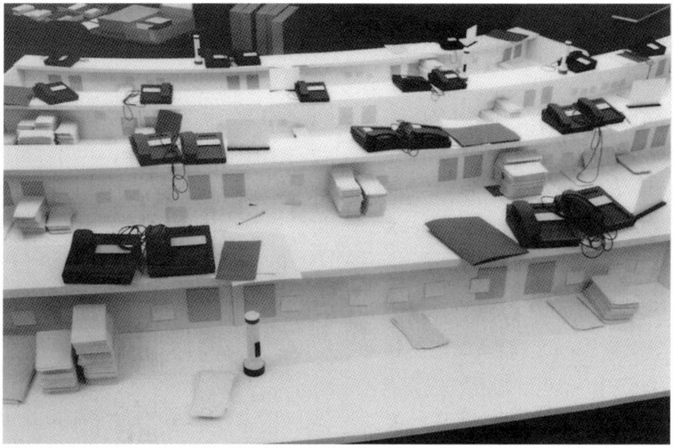

Poll, Thomas Demand, 2001– courtesy Esther Schipper Gallery, Berlin.

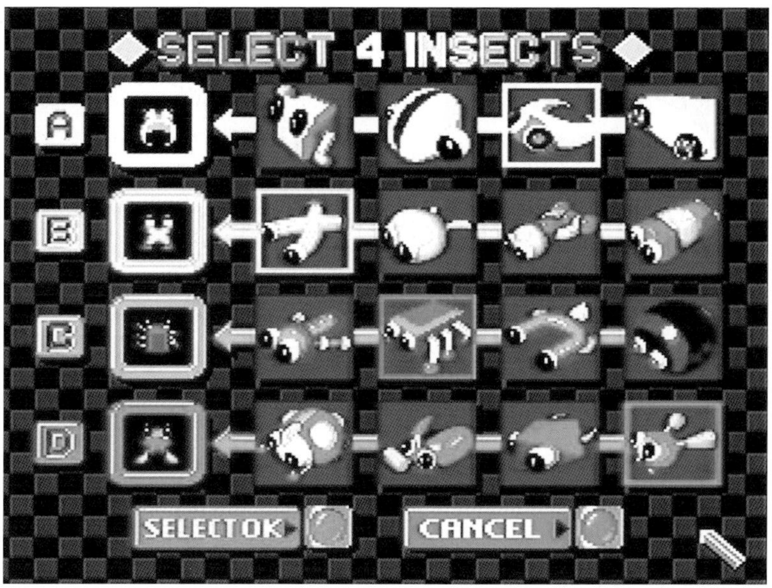

Select 4 insects/ Music Insects, Toshio Iwaï, 1992.

diabolic—Plato doesn't say diabolic, but close to that—because it presents itself for what it is not, it is pretence, a simulacrum, a visual sophistic. Strange declaration! Do you know many people who were mistaken as they looked at a painting, and took it for its model? It is totally implausible, however, it's from that paradigm that thought on the image has unfolded in the West. The virtual tries to create Plato's nightmare, an image that would have made the whole reality enter itself, including the reality of the one contemplating it. With the era of the virtual, we have entered the image, literally speaking.

Many television images are of that type: they virtually have no referent, they function in close circuit, on a loop, and only refer to themselves. Television generates a system of values, a system of "culture", or non-culture. It produces, in a way, its own referent that is strictly televisual. "The tele children": the phrase is not bad. Those who appear on the screen, only appear there as metonymies of the televisual system. There are less "icons", which would infer that they were still the images of something, than idols, meaning "images" freed of all references to anything else but themselves, drawing their whole reality from that lack of supply. Images that have become more real than any other reality whose images they would be.

But we would be wrong to say that about all the images produced by our culture. It is not the case in cinema, or at least, not a certain cinema, and that is why it was important to remind us of the density of the cinematic image...

Isn't density another name for beauty?

One of the questions I ask myself, and for which I don't have an answer, is why "virtual reality", for example, special effects, are so ugly... And I don't believe it's enough to just reply: because we are not used to them yet. I don't know if there is a simple answer to that question, but first, one should perhaps specify the question itself. It is not the ugliness of those "effects" which would make them non-artistic... I don't want to suggest here that cinematic work or artwork in general, should be submitted to the sole criterion of "beauty" in order to determine how artistic it is. I believe that to leave the criterion of beauty and replace it by a reflection on art, as has happened in the twentieth century is legitimate... However, I wonder if that renunciation is not partially based on a misunderstanding.

Beauty has been essentially rejected, I think, because one saw in it the category *par excellence* of a normative aesthetics which pretended to be able to tell us what is art, or what it should be. But, because aesthetics cannot be normative, one has concluded a bit too quickly that all reference to beauty was superfluous, or even misplaced, in art. But is that the case? It seems to me that the rejection of all notion of beauty shares the same presupposition as the traditional philosophy of art, according to which beauty is *the* artistic category *par excellence*: and so, to reject an *a priori* definition of art, and with it, a prescriptive approach, is to reject the category of beauty being applied to it. But what if beauty is *only one* of the possible categories in the analysis of art? I actually believe that is what's true… thus, that the only thing one could say is that beauty is only a category of art, next to a lot of others… Therefore one could, or rather, one should establish a "table of artistic categories"—I am not saying "aesthetic" for aesthetics is only an era of thought on art—a table of artistic categories which would include "beauty" but also lightness, vigor, intensity, balance, grace, etc., (and, of course, their opposites). For I don't think that beauty has a status different from that of the other concepts. It does not designate a normative "super category", or, at least, it is not more normative to talk about beauty than to talk about lightness or strength. It is not because beauty includes an appreciation or an evaluation that it is not a descriptive concept. To talk about "beauty" is to describe properties or qualities of the world itself, obviously in reference to some axiological principles. To say of someone that he or she is "brave", is indissociably to describe her, let's say, and formulate on her a value judgement. If one agrees with that, then there is no longer any reason to exclude beauty from the analysis of art, even contemporary art. To talk about "beauty" concerning contemporary works, is not to go back on the old normative aesthetics which consisted in saying that following certain rules was sufficient (I simplify) for an artist to be accomplished.

That said, there isn't probably a more difficult concept in philosophy than "beauty". One doesn't know how to define it. One of its aspects, which is not at all a definition, is, as Plato said, that it reveals itself to us *exaiphnès*, suddenly. Beauty reveals itself suddenly when it does. It grabs us. And when it reveals itself to us that way, for example, in an art piece, it seems to us that it depended on almost nothing, that it is a miracle, a balance. Thus, beauty has a singular way to appear, to show itself. But, as to saying what that appearing is the appearing of... It depends, obviously, upon the kind of thing one talks about: the beauty of a flower is not of the same order as that of a face or a painting… It is the opposite of what Plato said; there is no possibility to gather that under a unique form, an idea. But the difficulty to formulate what is common to all of that, the fact that there is no beauty as absolutely singular, the suddenness and unpredictability of its revelation, all of that contributes in persuading us that beauty, like other artistic qualities is almost impossible to premeditate, thus to fabricate. There is in beauty, a per-fection which doesn't demand any action, any "faction", any *facere*, any doing (*faire*). One shouldn't even say of beauty that it is "perfect" (*parfait*) if per-fect means "done through and through" (*fait de part en part*). There is always a dimension of unexpected or un-anticipatable in the—imperious—way it shows itself. That is the reason why there is also room for beauty in cinema—less so in television. Then, it is a question of knowing if, for example, in special effects, beauty can happen... From the moment an image is totally made, totally manufactured, thus where there is no longer room for the non-premeditated, is there still room for beauty? In any case, it remains for me an enigma to discover why special effects are so ugly...

> *But isn't beauty something which petrifies us, and thus, would suspend time, while art today is rather about developing artistic propositions involving active time, shared time in that relationship of the work and/or the artist to the spectator? There, in those interactive devices, it would appear that it's about another relationship to the work, for the one who is looking is not outside the work, but is an interactant-subject present in the work which, by virtue of an interpretative posture, will act on the work, will be part of the work. And who actualizes it, in a way, by taking part in its realization.*

That's possible. You describe here particular art pieces; perhaps it is a more general movement. But I wonder if that interactivity hasn't always existed. The idea of a spectator is a deceptive idea. What I mean is that the spectator who went to see a Greek tragedy, also took part in the festivity and celebration the show was part of. The spectator is always also a participant, which is what I tried to suggest by using the concept of "play", for example. I wonder therefore if that demand on the part of the contemporary artist, that the person whom the art is aimed at takes an active part in the advent of the work (or what is no longer really a work of art) is not something which pushes to its conclusion a logic which has always been in the art.

And what about architecture? Shouldn't we say that circulating inside the "art work" is part of that work? It's true that contemporary art has multiplied those interactions, for example in some forms of theatre, where the spectators are on stage. It is an attempt to make more porous the difference between the artist and the spectator, as well as between the artwork and what is not the artwork. Certain art works of Land Art can be mentioned, for example, those trees in which Giuseppe Penone finds their previous stages from their lineage: is it art or is it nature?

I'd like to go back on my previous question and that modification which happened in the reception of the artwork and the presence to the work in those contemporary propositions with devices in which the spectator is asked to become immersed: at the same time—as a spectator—one is in that real body which is ours, but also one is in a kind of virtual presence when one enters the universe of the artwork. A kind of dividing in two, of co-presence which confronts us with the perception of suspension of time, as you said earlier about beauty and, also, about play.
But, in that universe where we are challenged, our existence would no longer be fictitious, as when we project ourselves in the cinema, but it would also become "pragmatic" since we are able to act concretely there, and we have become "spect-actors".

I agree with that, with the slight reservation that those works push to the limits a tendency that is already there in art, in all art. Take a painting, for example: to see a painting is to glance at it, to clear a way of visibility that is neither entirely stipulated, nor entirely free. What is true is that the philosophy of art has not reflected a lot on that, but the artists themselves have thought about it in their practice for a very long time.

In those contemporary practices, which offer devices for crossing, for meeting, and circulating, it seems to me that the artists try to generate another experiencing of reality which wouldn't pass by the reality of our daily life, but would rather be a deviation from daily life, involving the spectator in order to provoke another way of looking at the world.
The artist would be an operator whose critical work emphasizes the concrete processes of the manufacturing of the image. Hence, an actualization of the experiencing of reality, as "work"(travail) of art. Not to say the reality, but to produce a possible reality (a virtuality, another experience).
I'd written down something about those notions of real-virtual we've talked about, which leads me to that question of the relationship between the experimental and its visible state. What I mean is how do we go from the experimental to the visible?
"To no longer define the image as image but as intermediary between image and object, in which the image becomes process, meaning it has its genesis and its end between the two, because of the inter-acting which will make the link".

What images are you thinking of? Those of "virtual reality"?

Not only the virtual images, but also the relationship that art maintains with play in its (re)creative form which, in a way, places the spectator in a kind of virtuality (in the sense of a promise, a possible).

I would however make a distinction between installations, where there is no image involved, and devices of virtual images, where you effectively interact with the image. It is not the same thing, for in an installation, the location of the installation is important. Almost always. Thus, it means that there is something that is already there that the artist welcomes.

In all virtual processes we have something else, or so it seems to me. One tips over in a world that would purely be an artifact, and consequently which would no longer be a world.

And it is also true that some positions of contemporary art consist in reducing as much as possible the distance between art and life, art and non-art. For example, by creating spaces to live in right in the middle of the exhibition space, where the spectator is invited to drink, eat, rest, and inhabit the space. It's a question of offering a new sensory, spatial and temporal experience that, in a way, sends us back to our existence.

Dubuffet started a movement of art towards daily life. Is that movement going to carry on? It is still as necessary? Didn't it have, originally, an essentially critical bearing, so that when that critique loses its edge, its relevance lessens? Or, on the contrary, is art going to join daily life even more, at least in some of those forms? I don't have any answer to those questions.

I was not talking specifically about daily life, but rather about the question of reality. Doesn't art, which works through those devices on constructions of time, rather try to re-appropriate for itself the question of reality—mitigating that way, a certain mediatic de-realization of the world—with that active participation of the spectator in the art works?
Doesn't it try to reintegrate in the artwork the body of a spectator who now is no longer a mere witness, or a virtual body but who seeks—with that active participation of the spectator—to make another experience happen from the reception of the work and of the world ('post-mediatic") which engages him as a watcher.

While the media want to communicate to us some "real time", some immediate, I think some artistic practices can give us back the sense of the ephemeral. Art involves temporalities that are much more diversified, stratified, difficult to describe, all those modalities of time, which are those of our experience of the world. You are right to say there is in the way some video installations, for example, reclaim and divert images relating to the media and make them echo the time we "bring" into the exhibition place, a time which cannot enter any format, a critical bearing, undoubtedly in the same way as setting up a ready-made in an exhibition room for Duchamp. Critique on art separated from daily life, on one side, political criticism on the other...

I was talking about the form of art with an interactive device in which one tries to involve the spectator with propositions of situations to experiment with. Hence that notion of "spect-actor" who becomes an "inter-actant", the author of the narrative which he is in the process of actualizing, of the work he is in the process of experiencing.
One could find something similar in video games. There is at the same time virtuality and reality for there is that body of the player who is going to step in with his mouse or his stick to create a virtual world. And that is no longer only virtual, for the ergonomy of the video game aims at generating pleasure, stress, challenge, etc... which are also part of the experience of play.

Yes, but I intervene on something whose possibilities are all entirely imposed. Nothing happens in a video game. The possibilities are perhaps of an unlimited order, by virtue of a combinative, but nothing can happen which depart from the rules of the program. In that regard, the world is certainly not a big computer, nor God a big programmer, whatever Leibniz thinks.

Any work of art worthy of that name is unpredictable: it opens a horizon of possibilities that did not exist before it. I'll give you a counter-example. One day, I was abroad and a woman, whom I'd just met, informed me that her husband was a painter. I asked her what type of painting he did. She replied: "It's halfway between Mondrian and Pollock." I wondered: "What is half-way between Mondrian and Pollock?" I couldn't see it at all. I couldn't see because I was looking for something really original. The answer was much simpler, and trivial. When I met the husband and I discovered his paintings, there was no mystery. What he was painting was truly something between Mondrian and Pollock: it was a Mondrian-like grid covered with splashes of paint in the manner of Pollock's action painting... This example is undoubtedly extreme, but anyway, it's one of what painting cannot be. I don't know what painting is, but at least I'm sure it is not that.

I cannot see for the moment—contingent on an evolution impossible to predict—what in the video game would really create the conditions for art, would go beyond the stage of commercial product, gadget.

When I talk about video games, I'm not thinking about those manufactured products one finds on the market, but about the model of the video game used by artists or film directors in their own device to give it a ludic aspect and introduce other narrative temporalities (than those, for example, we mentioned with the "central conflict theory"). On the model of the game, they try to generate other experiences, taking their inspiration from video games, with no unity of time, or chronological progression, where the only common denominator between all those stories is the author-narrator-character.

You're thinking about directors like Gus Van Sant?

I was also thinking about artists in visual arts who, with that work on time—and I'm not saying it's always successful—try to make something happen that we didn't see and which would perhaps be there, in the things. Thus, to produce another information.

For my part, I wouldn't say "information"...

But it would be understood as in-formation, another experience of reality.

Well, I agree, when the processes of the video game, like all other reality of our world, like TV images, those of fashion and advertising, are taken up in a form which is an artistic form. What is an artistic form? A very little element of an answer is that it is a form that makes something happen, which attracts our gaze and which, by attracting it, transforms it. Every artwork has, as its characteristic, that it teaches us how to look at it, how to approach it, how to go over it. It gives itself through a shape that implies, in order to be seen, that our gaze adjusts. Proust said it about Impressionism: not only can we no longer look at classical painting, but we cannot either look at the world itself in the same way before and after. That is the character of event, of causing-an-event of all artwork. I think that is the essential, and that it belongs to the fundamental experience we have of art.

So, from the moment the images, wherever they come from, including "virtual reality" or video games, are taken up in an artistic form which makes us think, nothing can set them against providing real "experiences" in the way one could talk about all art as Rilke talks about poetry: "verses are not feelings but experiences."

Experience is what throws into a crisis our understanding and our previous apprehension of things, what forces us to judge them (*krinein*) differently. Then, the video games, the fashion images, the TV shows, nothing is external to art if it is taken up in a form and if that form carries forward a true experience, I mean one susceptible to throw into a crisis our certainties, our conditioning, our routines. I believe the main notion here is that of form. If all of that is taken up in art, it is taken up in a "thinking form", as Godard said, and if it thinks, the form makes us think, it calls for a critical gaze, it forces us to look differently, it provokes a crisis of the gaze.

We are back to the question of knowledge through art that we could question anew with that question of the crisis of the gaze.

There is always a critical dimension in art that calls for our judgement and our knowledge. *Krisis*, yes.

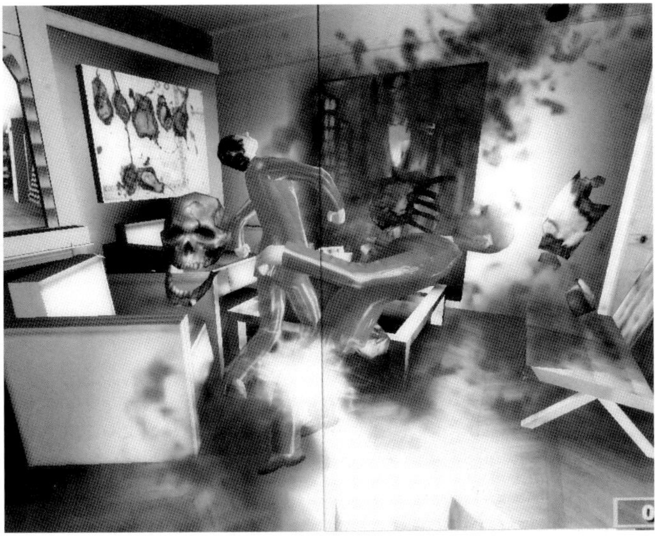

kolkoz.org / Level 1 : the secret flat, Kolkoz, 2002 - courtesy galerie Emmanuel Perrotin.

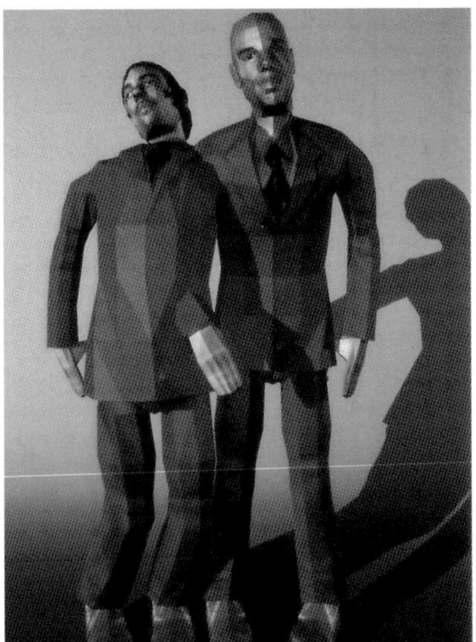

Players: kolkoz / V 1,0, Kolkoz, 2002 - courtesy galerie Emmanuel Perrotin.

ART AT STAKE OR THE DIVERSION OF TIME

The relationship that art maintains with video games is first of all its relationship to play, referring to the notion of play in general, and to the changes that the ludic value has generated in the reception of the work since the advent of postmodernity, by establishing a new spectator relationship to the narrative: interactivity. Consequently the spectator has become a player.

However, numerous diversions of the video game have taken place with art, particularly in the way we play. In artistic devices there is no addiction but propositions of interactive experiences. There is no goal to the game and the player is not induced to face trials or to solve mysteries, only to explore new forms of narrative structures destined to discover a universe or a theme, outside any context of competition. Let's take, for example, the role plays which characterize some games based on power, ambition, etc., not to mention the strategy which consists in never going down in the esteem of one's fellow citizens (for it all happens in a community of players). In video games based on role play, the destinies of the characters and the possibilities of courses belong to the program, not to mention that the values extolled are those of the law of the market. When art reclaims those games' devices, the characters are *real persons* who obviously also obey constraints of situations proposed by the artist—who uses the ludic protocol to diffract the narrative by inventing an interactive spectator—but situations which also remain open on the unknown since submitted to the experience of the game proposed by the spectator/player. That interactive process is about a situation of experiencing in which the spectator/ player can intervene on the characters' destinies and write their story.

Hence a questioning of the use of narrative time in video games which concern art.

In video games, what is interesting in the narrative field is its arborescence, for in the game's mechanism there are many more possible scenarios than in a film. For example, time is linked, here, to a multiplication of the possible courses where one experiences in accelerated motion a certain number of events. The value of time in ordinary respites is no longer used. These journeys are also found in art pieces through the meandering of the characters, of the man in the city (as in the exhibition *Game over city*). Counter to video games, the unfolding of the course is no longer strategic, time is not graded with a purpose in sight, but is about a progression which emphasizes the contradictions and the polysemy in the choice of the journey, tracing unusual routes which destructure the modes of temporality of the narrative, producing events happening in the aleatory mode, and no longer graded according to a chronological and causal criterion. At any time, the scenario can change or open onto a dead end.

What has fundamentally changed, through video games, in the apprehension of the game, is the notion of Internet, of playing in a network. There it is still another time, through persistent universes with multiplayers on line, and a virtual world that exists and changes permanently, independently from the player. With the help of technology, one also has to take into account the evolution of the game these last 2 or 3 years, for, with telecharging and portable games, the invention of the PSP (PlayStationPortable) and above all, the XBox, we are again experiencing a rupture. To play it is no longer necessary to be stuck in one's house, via the Internet, but with the Wifi we are mobile and able to play anywhere any time. We no longer play at home but everywhere in the world, with players in total immersion, as offered by games like MMORPG (Massively Multi-player Online Role Playing Game).

But in what world are we playing? One could say that this question of game underlines the political dimension of that appropriation and the diversion of the video games that the artists will operate. Let's not forget the "network" spirit, the community, a culture of exchange developed with the use of free software at the time of the advent of persistent universes, transforming the video game into a new popular art that some have called "the 10th art". But this reference to "game culture" in contemporary art—that one could call the expression of a "game art"—is a way to redefine another territory of references breaching what art history has codified as *high culture* (elitist culture) in comparison to *low culture* (popular culture). In the context of contemporary art, these codes of what one calls elitist and popular culture aim at being reshaped and at abolishing those distinctions, limits and social hierarchy. Art, by reclaiming and diverting a mass entertainment like video games, operates an editing process on the fragments of a cultural phenomenon which takes its full meaning in a world confronted by its dematerialization. This editing concerns the look and the putting into narrative where the artist plays his role. So we could say that the temporal paradoxes developed in video games would be of the nature of the temporality of visions. Infiltrated onto other playing fields by the artists, those paradoxes question the temporality in the experience.

GAMES: GENRE AND NARRATION

Video games develop several genres: adventure, fantasy games, reflection games, strategy games, immersion games (important for the question of time from the point of view of the player/visitor who immerses himself in the story) like the car games or simulation games. All those genres have been for the most part taken up, re-discussed, re-manipulated, and parodied by artists, except for strategy games that require fantastic scenarios. Those putting into narrative could have appeared to some as the possibility for a critique on the formatting of information through the media systems, with another way to approach the history we are told, for example, from some news items, as in Pierre Giner (*Keep the distance*—visual p.6).

Many have also taken their inspiration from film scenarios, or have re-appropriated the programs of games already existing (combat games like "Doom like" used mainly by Kolkoz and Tobias Bernstrup). It has also been used in *Super Mario Clouds* (visual p.87) by Cory Arcangel who has taken out all the visual components of Super Mario Bros except for the clouds that pass by non-stop. In another example, Palle Torson's *Sam*, the artist, inspired by the environment WorldCraft for Half-Life to build the background, has added prefabricated 3D objects, elements drawn from other games and web sites, where the player constructs the scenes and controls the action. Here, the player follows Sam, the heroine, a little girl out of control who, from her home to the school and beyond, starts to kill with no motives whatsoever, following her own impulses. What happens depends on the player, if he's willing to play. For Torson, what is interesting in this re-appropriation, is that the aggressive aspect of the game cannot be isolated from the violent reality in which we live.

Other artists have taken an interest in the question of the character as the starting point of a narration. In the case of *Ann Lee*, for example, Philippe Parreno and Pierre Huyghe have bought the rights in Japan of an unused manga drawing and have claimed it to create a generic character called Ann Lee, which will be used by several artists in the manner of those recurrent characters in role plays like Lightning, the heroine, appearing in ten versions of the game *Final Fantasy*. Ann Lee has now become a totemic figure in contemporary art, a character, however, with no prior story.[1]

[1] When we said with Pierre Huyghe "Ann Lee is a sign," that meant: "I am a character without a story. Does a hollow character have a chance to exist?" Cf. *Peut-on exister sans produire de récit?* a conversation by Jean-Max Colard and Philippe Parreno, in *02*/June2006.

The important thing about this reference to video games for artists is not so much the confrontation with new technologies but the stakes they generate. First it was the desire to take part, to be fans while keeping a distance in order to divert and crystallize their look. For the Swedish Tobias Bernstrup, Palle Torson and Magnus Wallin, because of their thorough knowledge of games and the way they redirect them, it is for example the theme of the city which will be taken up as a fetish subject, the city as performance: the body in the city and the performance in a kind of interactive walk. For those artists who use the universe of the video game with, as common denominator the architecture and complexity of the occupation of space in virtual universes, it concerns the questioning of public spaces, urban life and how one inhabits it.

Tobias Bernstrup's work in particular is articulated around the urban space, the body and electronic music, and transports us in Potsdamer Platz, a symbol of the architecture of the year 2000, a project gathering architects from all over the world to create a city which doesn't resemble anything else, for in 2006, Potsdamer Platz is regarded as an unavoidable architectural prowess, a place nobody lives in, a place one only crosses for an interactive walk. In the 3D modeling in *Potsdamer Platz* (an alteration of the game *Unreal Tournament*) the character (the spectator/player) who strolls at night in the city is not represented in the image, but only "present' in the sound of his footsteps. He guides as a subjective camera, a device taken from network games (FPS: ["first person shot"]). For it is the player who sees, hears and walks in a dead city whose architecture is cold, submerged in an atmosphere close to the universes of science-fiction.

Let's also mention Felix Stephan Huber who offers, with *Reality Check One*, a game in Alexander Platz in Berlin, one of the places in the city well-known for its underground passages constructed after the war, which symbolizes the cities' dehumanization. There is a game on the basement and an underground game. Several clones of Tom Raider or Spider Man or The Hulk talk to us. The artist gives the power of speech back to the heroes, with words coming from *Ghost in the Shell*, or from the feminine heroine of the Matrix. Felix S. Huber also restricts his architecture with the use of a *text box.* As soon as we are close to the dividing walls, we can read a text which passes like film credits with meaningful words, at times enigmatic, on reality and the game's virtual space.

I will take another example of strolling with Pierre Huyghe's *Le Château de Turing*, presented at the Venice Biennale in 2002. It concerned a natural meandering which recounted the time of a walk through three rooms in an exhibition place invested by the artist. The Turing's Machine was the keynote of the exhibition, the ancestor of modern computers and the foundation of classic

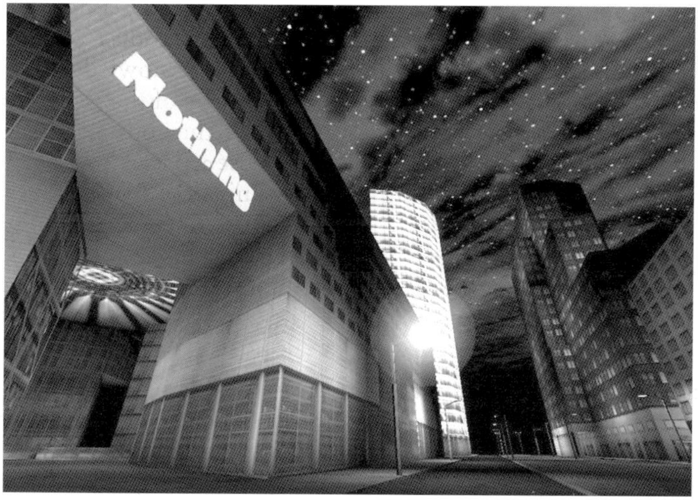

Potsdamer Platz, Thomas Bernstrup, 2001—courtesy Cosmic Galerie.

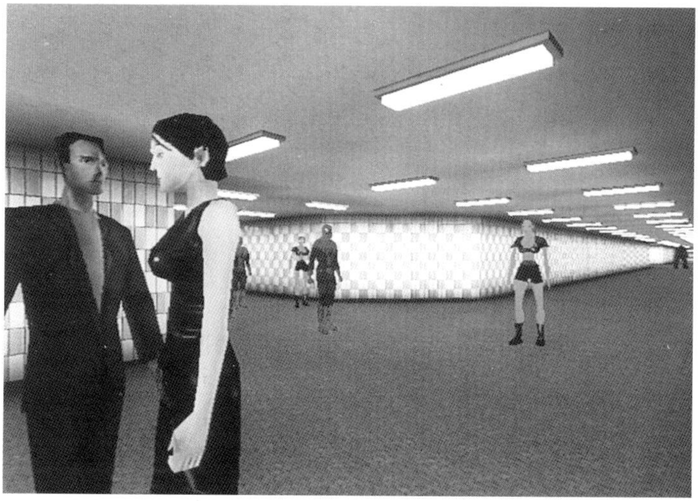

Reality Check One, Félix S. Huber, 2001.

I.T. and programming. Knowing that Turing's Machine is an imaginary machine, abstract and ideal, in which the entry ribbon is infinite and can be read in both directions, one can see the damage done to the logic of the program of the courses offered in video games, courses resting here on the impossibility to decide. In one of the exhibition rooms (*Atari Light*), there was a computer in a luminous ceiling programmed from the first interactive video game, the "Pong" (one of the very first video games played on the computer, which offered a kind of electronic tennis in its most simple form), from which some joysticks were hanging that the visitors used to play with, turning the light on in the exhibition room, and therefore the visibility of the works. So the script of the stroll was no longer programmed but caused by the chance of the game carried out by the visitors. It was also the question of demystifying the exhibition space and thus, the function of the space, by placing the playing field in the exhibition space.

Each time during those strolls, one is confronted by interactivity. For Pierre Huyghe with the Pong game, it was a matter of questioning it in its relation to artificial intelligence. That borrowing from video games of interactive devices is also found—still displaced and out of phase—in Toshio Iwai's work, who takes an interest in infography and computer games in order to develop musical and visual systems. In *Music Insects* (visual p.65), the visitor chooses, with the help of a rolling marble, the colors and trajectories of the virtual "insects" as well as the soundtrack.

SYNTHETIC LOOK AND TEMPORAL JUMP

What is representative of what one could see between 2001 and 2004 is a fascination for the reversibility of time that those games offered, no longer an aesthetics of games smoothed, linear and mono-directional, but an arborescence in the structure of the game itself, which led us to stroll in the generic cities for other encounters with time experienced. Bernstrup's work, for example. Felix S. Huber too, who had given shape to the encounter we had with characters such as the Marvel's heroes, or the heroes of films like Lara Croft (*Reality Check One*). Each time we met one, we ended up in their body, to follow wherever the adventure was going to lead us.

What came out of it was the question of narrative. Finally, the universe of the game and the digital images of the video were very cold, with a calculated image, flat and entirely aesthetic. Those interactive walks gave them back some depth, a time to stroll, although the one who played was also mechanized. At the time when all those images appeared, a few effects from cinema images were used, a few effects from automatic images—like automatic writing—through some software which were "broken into" so that it no longer was the commercialized program on hard disks, but the assemblage of several softwares re-manipulated and re-directed. Like all those artists, Bernstrup modifies, manipulates and re-directs for a result that resembles an immense tracking shot in a city or in empty spaces. For example, in *Potsdamer Platz*, one finds oneself at the top of one of the buildings, ready to fall. But one never sees the fall, only a reduction of the event where one finds oneself directly on the ground. A reduction of the action that synthesizes the vision, where one goes from A to C without having to mention B.

What video games contribute to is that synthetic gaze and the mechanisms of courses involving other temporalities which allow shortening of the time of the event and accelerating our visual acuteness while disturbing our codes of representation of the world. The combination of those artistic intentions is called "cinematic". Images combining cinema, animation and the statement of the video game in a clip or a short film.

That notion of reduction is evocative of the work of the painters on landscape and what the **Quattrocento** made of it through the frame, the window onto the world. Here the window is the screen, a new window onto the world. The difference is that in video games, the action is not one single viewpoint but several, seen through 3 or 4 cameras. So when the artists became interested in those modes of temporalities of the course (of the narrative), it was almost logical—because of technology—that the gaze was multidirectional straight away.

FROM DEPTH TO TIME, FROM SPACE TO EXPERIENCE

The reference to video games in the artistic context can be seen from the angle of the crisis of the look and that experiencing of new temporalities as propositions on depth and density in opposition to the "planet screen" (planète écran) and flattened world. I think here particularly about a Finnish artist, Pia Rönicke, who, through the question of architecture, tries in her films to change the relationship we have with perspective in real space. It's a question there of the importance of architecture that conditions our behavior in the city and modifies perhaps our *mental map*. A loss of orientation that could be necessary to think differently, to modify a habit.

Finally, through the computer screen, is it not still a landscape, as if through the **Quattrocento**'s window? A window onto the world but with the difference that today there is in reality a multitude of windows. In a contemporary sense, it seems to me it is worth having a look at Franz Ackermann, for that return to another kind of map and the way he looks at

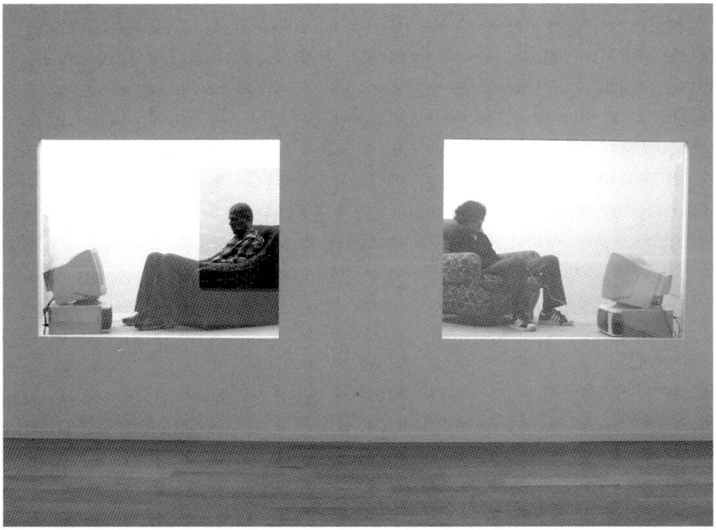

Kolkoz, view of the “Connivence” exhibition, biennale de Lyon, 2001.

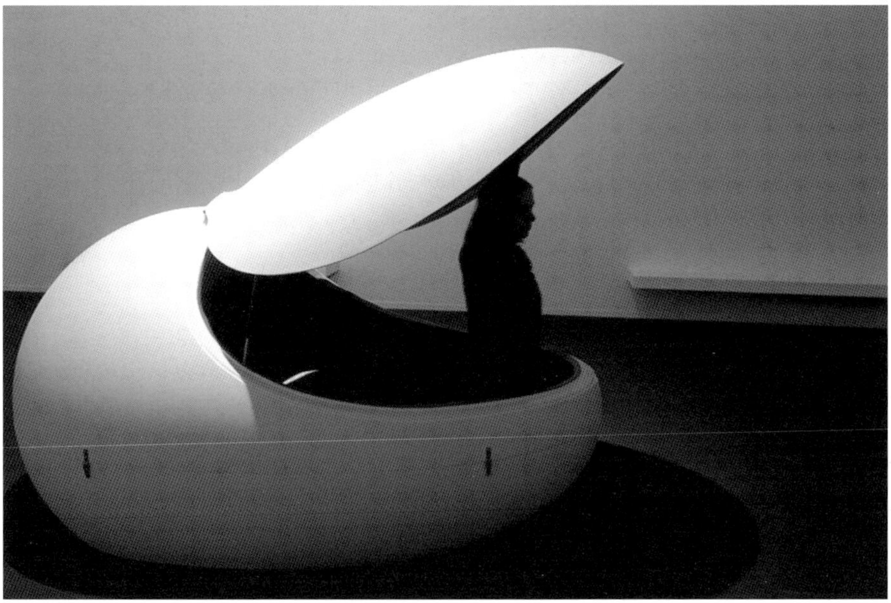

Derrière le monde flottant, Mathieu Briand, (“SYS*021.IsN*01/EsE-AcE.InR-ExR\Mic-EnE*4)- Musée d'Art Contemporain, Lyon, 2004.

cartography. He is interested in the figurative representation of the moment and, in order to create his paintings, he uses 3D images from photos he has taken. That artist proposes ruptures of the code of representation—like Monet had done with *Les Nympheas* by representing the ground almost as if from a bird's eye view. Propositions which go far beyond our peripheral vision, for example, with *Mental Maps*, made of geomorphologic maps of a city where the complex reality, made of photos, videos and various objects, pushes the spectator to read the image in depth, to become aware of the visible which surrounds him.

That multiplicity of the mediums is like strata which produce more density in the image, and perhaps, more sensuality. I'm talking here from a merely aesthetic point of view, and that would explain that return journey to painting. More density in the screen too. One notices today a return to physical elements, from drawing to animation. Thus, some reality, some tangible too, and body (forgotten in the virtual) which are the attempts at leaving behind that flattened world. I'm thinking here, for example, about Melik Ohanian's Ann Lee (*I am dreaming about a reality*), a cyborg programmed to dance and seduce to disco rhythms, which is offered to leave the virtual world in order to enter a tangible reality. But a bug interferes and the promise of entering reality is put to an end forever: "no database'. That fatal error of a lack of enough memory (because of too much information) is perhaps the prefiguration of our next "big *bug*".

This world through the window-screen and this "flattened world" in which we play are also our world, that of globalization. But this apparent flatness doesn't mean that we are flat, and the depth we find in art works—going back to the **Quattrocento** and its use of perspective—also comes from the spectator's time. Time as depth to come out of the flattened world.

IMMERSION TIME

With play, there is also another notion of time which steps in with the introduction of the spectator into an artwork where he ends up projecting himself into a story initiated by the artist. The fact is that the time for playing is a time for enjoyment, where one leaves behind one's own story, one's own temporality. To play, the spectator must be able to immerse himself in the game. A time for playing which is that of the exhibition, that time of appreciation of the artwork that allows the spectator to immerse himself in the system of vision proposed by the artist.

The notion of taking part has evolved enormously. The sensorial dimension, for example in Mathieu Briand depends on a very sensual participation, on an immersion (visual p.82). I could also mention Jeppe Hein, a

for reality, and reality, a space for game, they had recreated models of the interface of the game "Half Life", by imagining a game in network to generate a reflection both on architecture and on the ergonomy of game which explains the object of the relationship established between players and public. Their creation of modeling started then from a game that was only a pivot, an interface that was used to sway from one reality to another. Today, they do the opposite. They start from a holiday movie that they create models from, recreating design objects that they collect and appropriate, objects of desire, especially sofas, a first Mac etc.... It is therefore not only their characters—even though there is also the question of self-portrait—but it's especially the idea of introducing fiction from an ordinary film, such as a holiday movie, which is involved here.

In order to make reality even more like fiction, they will also modify, like a second stratum, the scale of reality by reducing it to 2/3 scale. One could go back here on the window we have talked about earlier which also reduces the field of vision. But that reduction is equivalent to a notion of lie, in the sense of transformation of a reality, where fiction-modification-reality-reduction of the scale = lie, meaning transformation. Which means that one is in a way forced to "cheat" with reality when one is in a code of representation or even of narration, since reality is impossible to obtain. They extracted from their holiday movies ten minutes of creating models showing through those successive reductions of the action—from their holiday to the film and creating models—that simulation and lie are inherent to the re-transcription of reality.

Other artistic experiences play on those tenuous relations between reality and fiction by leaning on the social and political reality of the world transmitted by information and media. It is the reality of the political narrative that is questioned here, of the artist and his commitment to society. Today political narrative touches—especially for a contemporary generation of American artists—the commitments of the country and the protest against the war, or denounces advertising. In a way, a digestion of those last thirty years. For example, Jenny Perlin, an artist who uses, among other things, animation, but who has especially found and reworked archives in McCarthyism she salvaged from her lawyer relatives. Among those documents, some from people who were spied on, as in our society people who are victims of phone tapping, formulating that way a critique of that witchhunt which was some kind of phantasmagoric obsession than some kind of reality. Those archives give an account of small talk where, after transcription, nothing transpired other than the banality of those conversations. Transcribed and animated in her play *No Transcription*, those banal conversations reveal how the fantasy of the danger of spying modifies the relation to reality and is the sign of a society that is turning schizophrenic. A sign which, though it originates in American society, has

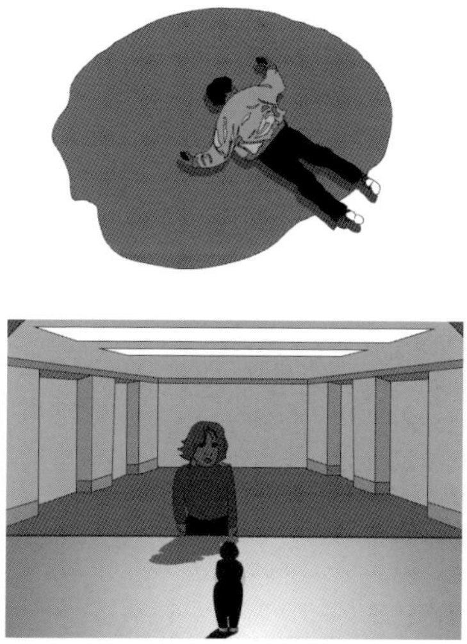

Rouge total, Virginie Barré and Stéphane Sautour, 2001—Animation film (4 mins), color, sound, Camera Lucida - courtesy Galerie Loevenbruck, Paris.

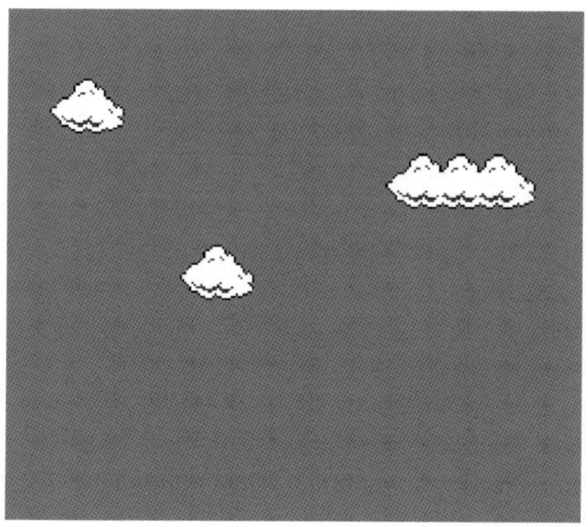

Super Mario Clouds v2k3, Cory Arcangel, 2002 - Hacked game cartridge, Nintendo Playstation variable dimension - courtesy galerie Thaddaeus Ropac, Paris, Salzburg.

contaminated us a bit. What finally comes out of the play is that an attentive re-reading of those archives allows to come to the surface information on those events that had been transmitted to us as a lie. A putting into narrative for a story which has no foundation in reality, only a production of proofs based on a fantasy. Therefore, it is not so much the video games which make things virtual and un-real but also the world of information in which we are plunged in spite of ourselves (and not immersed which is on the side of play, choice and art).

That work of an artist who inquires into the "forgotten" archives of our recent history—an investigation which could be that of a journalist or a historian—by confronting the facts and information in relation to other narratives, offers another reading which is equivalent to an implicit critique of the information which is transmitted to us. With *No transcription*, Jenny Perlin takes up a story cast aside in the private archives belonging to her family and not the archives found in libraries or official institutions.

What is also significant in that work is the desire to reanimate those "forgotten" objects or stories to build the structure of Culture or official History. A phenomenon one also finds—like a slightly post-modern return—in the use of the traditional techniques of cinema like Super 8, or in the desire to revisit the political events which happened a few decades ago. It is a subject which has already been commented upon in contemporary art and which refers to abandoned data one re-infiltrates. Another form of narrative is established here, the exploration of that of cinema and that of the universe of video games. Now, those researches on other narrative forms draw from the narrations of past facts, and also from abandoned techniques and technologies one re-animates in the contemporary world. Facing a reality increasingly assertive, mediatically telling and more and more fantasized, the notion of fragment takes on all its meaning. The fragment allows the reversal of an order, to disconnect the rules of the game. It favors the multiplicity over the sum as the artists, bringing into play other processes of editing for new offers in reality, put forward.

TIME, MEANDERINGS, THE EXPERIENCE OF LOOKING

The position of the spectator immersed in an exhibition visit outside the walls introduces another form of narrative into the meandering, a possible tracking game in the city which refers to older and more ludic practices of game in the city one has completely forgotten about. It concerns a spatio-ludic temporal notion which, as an adult, we have lost, unlike the children, with that tendency we have to fix the objects in their functionality. This rupture is also the opportunity for disruptions in our way to apprehend, to see. The tracking game in the city, or any artistic intervention in the city, tackles the political dimension of art while making of the city a playground the people can re-appropriate.

It is also the place for the unforeseen (un-fore(seen)) and the encounter (en-counter) like a percussion, a shock, meaning a time contradicted in relation also to what one is used to see. I'm also talking about that notion widely criticized today, the idea of the mainstream in art and in fashion. It's the desire to have that kind of percussion, events that break up the time in our daily life. To play on the word "en-counter", "counter" implies a proximity and a relation to time which induces a present to things, the here, the now, and no longer a fantasy on infinity, like in the virtual. It is also a relation to the body, the encounter of the body confronted by another vision that cuts the ground from under our feet.

One could talk here about the shock of looking. I think about what was said of Duchamp's "Urinal", a kind of object which strikes sharply, which catches us off guard in relation to what we are used to see. But it is also in the order of the gesture, the unforeseen and the play. Duchamp is a player on words, and he makes a game of each situation. We are back to what we said about playing and about the child who comes to disturb the status quo of the look. Playing is also the surrender of the body, of the self. I come back to the idea of immersion for, here too, one needs to completely surrender and not to fear being scared. For that encounter linked to chance to happen, there is necessarily a meandering and that surrender seems important to me because it can allow the unforeseeable to occur.

Playing allows one to lose oneself, but one cannot delude oneself for it is invented by somebody, that's the limit and the problematics. For in the end, rules are constructed from the beginning, but what is important is how one enters the rules and reinvents them. Here one plays and one loses oneself in the playing. In meandering, the visual encounter or the visual shock is much more improbable and depends upon chance, since one doesn't know one is going to be confronted with a new representation. On our incapacity or difficulty to lose ourselves, one shouldn't forget everything is done for us to lose ourselves less and less, everything is classified, listed. There have been several artistic works which have shown that, by showing the other side of that cartography and that city grid, latticed, which implies that nobody can get lost, or hardly. For example, Pia Rönicke and her urban fictions (*Cell City*, 2003, [visual p.35]).

NEW MODALITIES OF NARRATIVE

The link between video game and animation is the cinematic device that proposes synthetic narrative structures for the "flash" courses whose purpose is a faster immersion into the game so that a clearly defined and possible action can really start. Like cinematics, animation compresses time, it is a bit like the "clip" of a vision of the video game. What interests me is the concept developed by artists who, through that reduction sometimes to 5 minutes, induces other codes of representation with a synthetic and multidirectional look.

With the device of animation, we no longer are fixed on a programmed time, but on a time which also indicates the idea of gesture. One goes back to a practice of drawing, precise, short, focussed, with the desire to simplify to the maximum, to come out of the visual peripheries and pollutions to reach a precise moment in our time, which can be that of our daily life or that of daydreaming.

The history of animation film is rich with a long story of more than a century that has influenced the twentieth century and the artworld, with its constantly renewed creativity. At the end of the nineties, one witnesses an evolution of the definition of animation which breaks free from a certain ultra realist aesthetics with a return to practices less technological and more intimate. Artistic creation today is traversed and re-invigorated by a formidable activity linked to forms of animation films whose creators use all the actual potentials of graphic manipulation. The appearance of those new modalities which combine drawing to movement, is the consequence of a mastering of several technological layers which, from the interactive stroll to animation, to the cinematics of video games, passing by the culture of videoclips, leads us to consider them as the expression of a new narrativity.

The definition and status of the animation film are often uncertain, difficult to qualify. The notion of unfinished or the notion of a thought quickly formulated often characterizes animation works. At the cross between drawing, collage technique and editing, the artists find themselves at the heart of a free creation, without a framework and with images that flow ad infinitum. Animation induces de facto a reflection on the experiencing of a moment. A look on the city, a trial transmitted by the media, moments of nature in mutation, scenes of traditional life, holiday movies, a dog on a beach. A selection of small scenes of life full of humor and tenderness.

Technically the drawings are produced by hand then scanned and reproduced by computer. One goes back, there, on something artisanal but with the vigor of the image and movement which animates it. In these days of crisis of representation, it has really reinvigorated the video genre, a part of which went towards cinema, the other towards animation. Why? Because historically, animation could have taken two turnings. The starting point was theatre, for example with Mélies and his fetish actress, it was magic and theatre. Very quickly though the evolution pushed it towards wide-audience cinema, especially towards Hollywood. What is interesting in the end is that animation—except for cartoons—chose to stay on the fringe, and thus has been enormously enlivened by a work on the film, on film stock itself, on drawing and movement, finding again a certain youthfulness concerning what is represented.

There was little humor in the universe of video games, or more exactly, there was little distanciating, for the stakes at the time it crystallized, around 2001-2003, were more in the phenomenon of the game and the preoccupations of a new temporality, as we have said earlier. There, one finds a lot of parody, of caricature linked to the political world. For example at the time of Emile Kohl, who came from caricature drawing, the genre of animation concerned the point of view of political parody, which is today re-infiltrating the field of contemporary art with a kind of denunciation of the political, especially with the Bush era which activates it, with American artists (for example, *Polle*, by Thomas Demand, 2001—visual p.65).

The game and ludic aspect in art could appear to be dependent upon a will to "regress" in comparison with a "high" image one has of art, and that, in the end, nothing is more enjoyable than to see a play by Robert Fillioux which decodes the word and becomes a game, a puzzle, a witticism. One could also mention the relations established between comics and contemporary art, a form some people call "puerile". For example the very stylized drawings, aesthetically close to comics, of Virginie Barré borrow from manga, American comics, Pop Art and are reproduced in the digital video *Rouge Total* (2002), made with Stéphane Sautour (visual p.87 and *Je sentais...*, 2004, visual p.125). Or Gilles Barbier in *Sans titre* (*La fabrication de la mousse*), 2005—(photo p.13) who introduces comic bubbles and messages, "corrections of reality" to the characters, which really shows that the reference to that form of expression is perhaps not as "puerile" as it appears.

We are again here in a re-definition of "high culture" and "low culture". Through the analysis of philosophers or exhibition curators, art critics or the gaze the artist casts on society, we have three possibilities of approaching a work of art. The hyphen is the ludic which is a way to keep one's distance, to move reflections onto another field than the more intellectual one. That would be a part of the answer. Another would be the marriage of "high culture" and "low culture" with Pop Art, media art, television art ... Internet too, in reality. All those new technologies have modified the time and space of communication by speeding up the transmission of messages, multiplying the technological processes of representation, and establishing, with the virtual, another type of interface to reality which has modified our perception. The acceleration of mediatised time, which has joined real time by modifying our relationship to the world and to knowledge, also leads us to reconsider the relationships established between time, narrative and lived experiences.

Elephant, Gus Van Sant, 2003 (John, played by John Robinson) - Teenager framed.

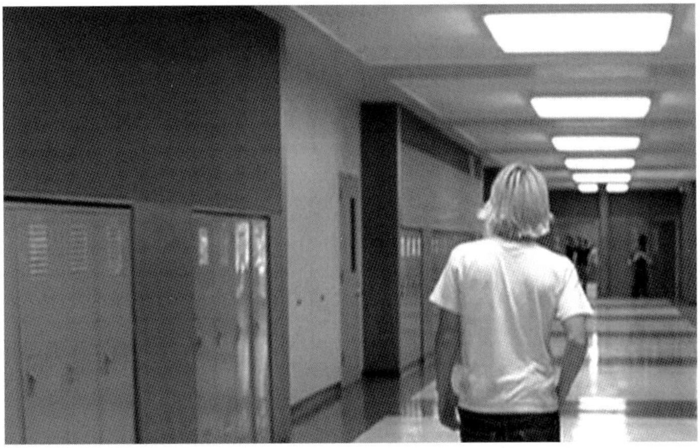

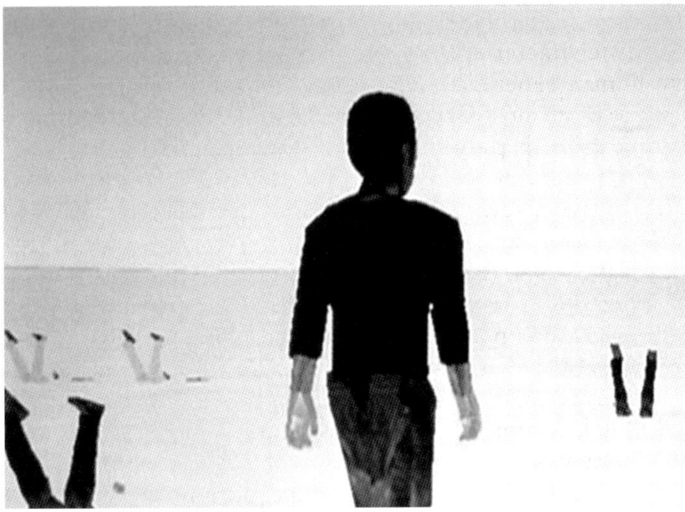

Elephant, Gus Van Sant, 2003 - Free play.

CINEMA UNDER THE INFLUENCE OF PLAY

LUDIC REFERENCES AND THE STATE OF PLAY IN CONTEMPORARY CINEMA

> It is a characteristic of *mimesis* to seek in the *muthos* not its fable-like nature, but its coherency. (...) To compose a plot is already to make the intelligible come out of the accidental, the universal out of the singular, the necessary or probable out of the episodic. (Ricœur, 1983: 70)

This characteristic of the narrative—fictional or historical—to represent the human experience of time, discordant, by means of concordance, appears to be one of its most significant stakes. Indeed, the fictitious experience of time summoned through plotting seems to address "the necessity to throw an Apollonian veil on the Dionysian fascination for chaos" (Ricœur, 1984: 46-47). It is that same concordance, revealed in the chronological narrative, the omniscient narration and the causal series, that literary, then cinematic modernity wanted to tamper with—slightly in vain according to Ricœur. Contemporary popular cinema aggressively integrates narrative processes that, in comparison with tradition, redefine equilibrium by means of discordance[1]. When Ishaghpour observed relatively recently the imperatives of accessibility and readability which characterize the expectations of the spectator in these times of mass media proliferation[2], a slightly more convoluted principle seems to have presided over the recasting of the relationship between film and spectator in contemporary times: the ludic. The planetary explosion of the video game phenomenon is surely not foreign to that recasting. Ishaghpour immediately pointed at television; though it is

[1] In the mid-1990s, Cahiers devoted an article to that tendency. See Ostria, Vincent (1994). "Glissements progressifs du plaisir interactif", Cahiers du cinéma, n°476, february, p.65-68.

[2] See especially, "La télévision", in Cinéma contemporain. De ce côté du miroir, Paris, Editions de la Différence, pp.17-35.

impossible to disregard the direct influences of video games on cinema, the present contribution proposes to go beyond the trivial intersections in order to better distinguish the many occurrences of a cinema which seems always more permeable to the idea of play.

The period in question obviously corresponds to cinematic postmodernity, so the problematic approached here is not foreign to it. We have decided however to put aside one of its more salient characteristics, the "sur-allusivity", the exponential multiplication of intertextual intersections, and that despite the ludic potential of such intersections and the sometimes considerable role they play in several examples which will be given through this essay. That path of research would take up all the space available in order to be meticulously formulated, on the other hand, it generates quite a lot of interest and, even better, sometimes ends up in good hands[3]. Despite that exclusion, it is that ludic relation, and, by extension, the various modalities that construct it, which will be tackled here. Anticipated by Gardies as early as 1972 in his work devoted to Robbe-Grillet[4], the problematic of the "playful spectatorship" has been developed substantially more recently in Bernard Perron's work. Building up his analogy between cinema and the activity of play from Roger Caillois' original typology, Perron proposes the concept of the filmic game. Governed by a principle of regulation (the Calloisian *ludus*, in contrast to the *paidia*, the free and unbridled play), the filmic games are organized according to two fundamental characteristics of play stated by Caillois: the *ilinx* and the *agon*, meaning, respectively, the thrill of vertigo and the pleasure of competing. This distinction will come in handy to organize various narrative processes, but the main focus of this paper will be to question the more or less effective discordance put forward by these processes. That way we will be able to derive more easily the real stake governing contemporary narrative renewal.

The most obvious parallel between cinema and video game, beyond the various processes put in place by some films to echo the game, is summed up in an economic synergy, fed on projects easily adapted from one media to the other and simultaneous launches, a phenomenon already well-documented[5]. The upheaval

[3] Sébastien Babeaux's research seems particularly stimulating and rigorous, especially: (2004) *De la citation à l'interférence: croisements dans le film contemporain*, Montréal, Université de Montréal.

[4] More particularly: "Vers un mode de rapport nouveau avec le spectateur: le ludique", Alain Robbe-Grillet, Paris, Seghers, p. 93-102.

[5] See in particular: Valletoux, Thierry (1995). "Le cinéma dans l'enfer du jeu", Studio, Dossier spécial jeu vidéo, n° 104, november, p. 116-121; Higuinen, Erwan, Charles Tesson (2002). "Jeux Vidéo. La nouvelle alliance du film et du jeu", Cahiers du cinéma, Dossier: "Cinéma et jeux vidéo: les nouvelles correspondances", p. 10-11, followed by a relevant interview with Christophe Ganz; Perron, Bernard (2004). "Plein jeux sur le cinéma contemporain", Actes du colloque Cinéma contemporain, état des lieux in Lyon, 2002 (sous la direction de Jean-Pierre Esquenazi), Paris, L'Harmattan, p. 293-308.

that the video game industry has imposed on the media landscape is accompanied by a certain tendency, for several commentators, to notice video game influences everywhere in cinema. Obviously, the examples of stories built around games have proliferated since *The Wizard* (Todd Holland) in 1989: *Brainscan* (John Flynn, 1994), *Level Five* (Chris Marker, 1997), *eXistenZ* (David Cronenberg, 1999) just to name a few. The intersections that interest us first and foremost operate on deeper levels. To begin with, video games seem to participate in a certain "impoverishment" of action or adventure film, the interest of those large scale movies being reduced to a series of spectacular scenes linked in a trivial way, at the expense of a global configuration craftily woven. Here video games, at best, take part in a tendency that has started way before its ascent, i.e., the recrudescence of the attraction in the cinematic production and, consequently, the proliferation of Odin's "new spectator" in movie theatres. However, this re-centering on an episodic nature does take part in a first effective reference to the video game. Today still, the ludic universes are organized in independent episodes, with each player probably going over it more than once. It is precisely that typical video-ludic experience which is evoked by the structure of *Groundhog Day* (Harold Ramis, 1993) and *Run Lola Run* (Tom Tykwer, 1998). The use of the knowledge acquired during a previous "game" by Phil, the protagonist in Ramis' film, clearly establishes a connection with video games. Even though the introduction to Tykwer's film only echoes the general notion of play and that the overlapping of the knowledge from one sequence to the next is not so clearly evoked, the same parallel is confirmed by the framing of the protagonist.

A second formal reference to video games is visible solely through the framing of certain scenes. The filmic/profilmic collusion that some spectators would have noticed in *Run Lola Run* is systematized in Gus Van Sant's film, *Elephant* (2003). In Lola's case, the lateral tracking shots which accompany the frantic run of the protagonist can be reminiscent of the flat scrolling of two dimensional games, but that type of shot is not unheard of in movies. The systematic use of the tracking shot which follows closely and rigorously the young people in *Elephant*, remains an oddity, and refers more directly to the virtual camera of three dimensional games which is situated imperatively behind the protagonist to accommodate the gameplay. *Rosetta* (Jean-Pierre and Luc Dardenne, 1999) proposes a similar framing, though more terse; the reference to games is undoubtedly non-intentional, even though the Dardenne brothers have purposely refined the narrative right back to its nucleus, focused on survival

(Benoliel, 1999: 48). In *Elephant*, the stylistic choice of the sequence shot, which leads the work to "a logic of circular action, in conjunction with an overvisibility of the image", according to Raymond Bellour (2004: 6), as well as the choice of the 4:3 format, reinforce the parallel with video games. The insistence of those "corridor shots" (visual p.92) that several commentators have noticed, allows us to better evaluate the relevance of this reference in the constellation of meanings that the film offers. The figure of the corridor is still very present in the realm of video games; the disappearance of the walls and ceilings in the video game effectively presented in the movie, is probably not fortuitous (visual p.92). Through this correspondence, Van Sant seems to reply to the media coverage of the event, which has found in a detail—the consummation of violent games by the killers—a reassuring explanatory element[6]. In the discordance of reality, video games are only one element among so many others, as demonstrated by the famous panning which accompanies the *Bagatelle in A Minor (Für Elise)* played on the piano by one of the future killers. When he introduces the game in that scene, Van Sant seems to point not to its potential effects for allurement, but to its liberating character.

Other recent framing techniques could be connected to video games. The extravagant camera movements simulated with the help of synthetic retain the same flexibility associated with the virtual camera of video games, free from a restricting material nature[7].

Another common principle, indebted to the all-including computer medium, will allow us to begin the study of strictly narrative processes that are not directly linked to video games. In his account of the "Cultural interfaces" characteristic of contemporary times, Lev Manovich emphasizes the importance of the database. Contrary to the narrative, the database doesn't link the contents imperiously, in accordance with some conception of the probable or the necessary; its operative principle rather favors accumulation. The confrontation of those two notions is embodied in an exemplary fashion in the video game phenomenon, where each performance invites the regulated combination of an ensemble of elements that determine the possible worlds of each game. Though the film theatres don't allow it to be actualized so concretely, that confrontation is evoked by the narrative configuration of several cinematic experiences. On that level, Peter Greenaway's work is undoubtedly the most significant. The ostensible purpose of the artist rests on the staging and questioning of a certain encyclopedist will

[6] Besides,Van Sant has underlined the determining character of that media coverage in the working out of the project.

[7] The effect is especially perceptible when, in *Fight Club* (visual p.99) or *Panic Room* (David Fincher, respectively 1999 and 2000), for example, the camera slides inside a bin, in the handle of a kettle or even in a keyhole.

exploited very early on in his filmography. *The Falls* (1980) is made up of 92 short biographies, corresponding to the persons whose surname starts with the letters "Fall", an apparently arbitrary selection amongst all those who would have been affected by the VUE (Violent Unknown Event). In *Vertical Features Remake* (1978), the encyclopedist's determination is expressed on two levels, first through the attempts at reconstructing a film attributed to Tulse Luper, *Vertical Features*, then, by the subject of Luper's film itself, which aims at being a collection of vertical lines drawn from the English landscapes by the camera. That insistence on the common object will become, incidentally, Greenaway's favorite method to integrate the same preoccupations on his more narrative efforts. Already foretold by the arbitrary numbering of the various objects in *Drowning by Numbers* (1988), this method is systematized in *Prospero's Books* and, more recently, in *The Tulse Luper Suitcases* (2003-2004, visual p.104) through the invasion of objects coming from the same series (Prospero's 24 books, Luper's 92 suitcases) and directly related to the encyclopedist project. Those irruptions break off the narrative and, through accumulation, repositions the work vertically to a certain degree. This "paradigmatic laying out" thus becomes a fundamental, organizing principle, eventually supported by baroque staging (*Prospero's Books*), the documentary framing of the fiction (*The Tulse Luper Suitcases*), or through the tiled arrangement of the shots now a characteristic of the director. Through all these aspects, Greenaway's films qualify as "*vertical features*".

Whether it refers to encyclopedist ambitions or, more specifically, to the database, the integration of such an explicit verticality in the narrative inevitably leads to a confrontation. Two examples, however, allow us to evoke a fiction that would be contaminated from the inside with this "paradigmatic laying out". The subdivision of the screen into four identical frames and, moreover, the organization of the imaginary world in four strictly parallel sequences of identical order and duration, confer to the project *Time Code* (Mike Figgis, 2000) a certain depth (visual p.104). The narrative device here involves the actualization of moments whose existence would traditionally depend on the spectator's imagination, or which would not even exist in the imagination of the "plot orchestrator" (Ricœur), since a narrative so rarely sheds light on each part of a continuous evententemential nucleus with the same intensity[8]. Werner Schroeter's film, *Deux* (2002) offers us a very different example of a narrative contaminated by verticality. Through the diptych Maria/Magdalena played by Isabelle Huppert, the director invites us to see

[8] Obviously this intensity is relative, in so far as in cinema, as in the interactive version of the film offered on DVD, the work on sound grades again the contents.

a collection of virtuous/decadent tableaux linked by accumulation and with no regards for causality.

The method that will hold our attention now is equally concerned with the accumulation of narrative propositions. But, while those propositions would gather in a coherent way in *Time Code*, and even in *Deux* (through their thematic kinship), the method in question rather implies the mutual exclusion of several possibles offered to the spectator. It no longer organizes the content under the modality of "and then", but rather works on "or else". In *Run Lola Run*, or in *Groundhog Day*, the alternative versions are the result of the protagonist's action, or the result of chance, behind which the narrative level hides. From one crossing to the next, the imaginary episode remains identical and comes into being according to the same rules, referring that way to video games, as we've seen. At the other end, the variations offered by *Three Lives and Only One Death* (Ruiz, 1996) and *Smoking/No Smoking* (Resnais, 1993), among others, presuppose the visible modification of the universe narrated by the plot orchestrator. Ruiz explains: "I've tried to work with stories, rather abstract I must confess, using what could be called a pentaludic model, or, to say it more simply, considering my protagonists like a 'troop' of dice" (1995: 19). In short, the plot orchestrator suddenly throws the dice, introducing an apparently arbitrary change in the imaginary universe (even though, obviously, he knows all of its facets). That cast of the die was already apparent in *Snakes and Ladders* (1980), which made the protagonists access a higher level (visual p.99). Even though a common territory exists—a unique set—in *Three Lives and Only One Death*, the sudden changes of personalities are not reduced to a pseudo-psychologic explanation; the four faces of the Mastroiani-die are shaken in the hand of the narrative level, which makes of the permutations, a fundamental narrative strategy. It is a very similar cast of the die which operates at each apparition of the title "or else" in the Resnais' diptych, who organizes however the variations much more rigorously (visual p.99). In any case the plot orchestrator comes to the surface, confirms his position as creator and, consequently, is re-doubled, staged.

From clear references to video games (episodic repetition, filmic/ profilmic collusion to imitate the video game presentation), we have noted processes which refer more generally to the meeting of the narrative and the IT medium (virtual camera, paradigmatic laying out), then to the notion of play itself (the narrative cast of the die). Those processes constitute, first and foremost, rules of configuration. After all, they only ask of the spectator to acknowledge the clever composition game of the narrative level. Generally, the examples mentioned so far refer to the

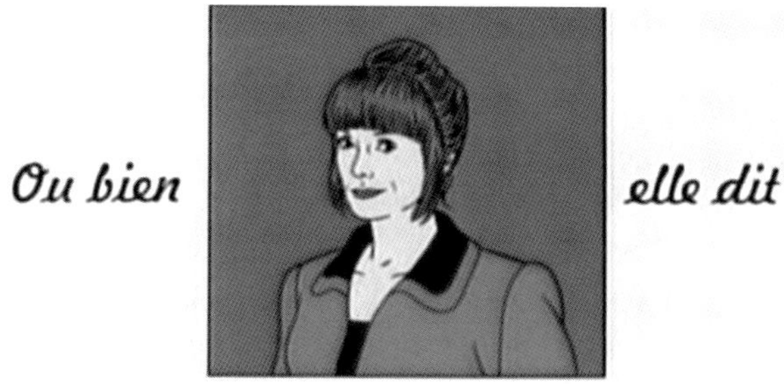

Smoking/No Smoking, Alain Resnais, 1993 - Or else...

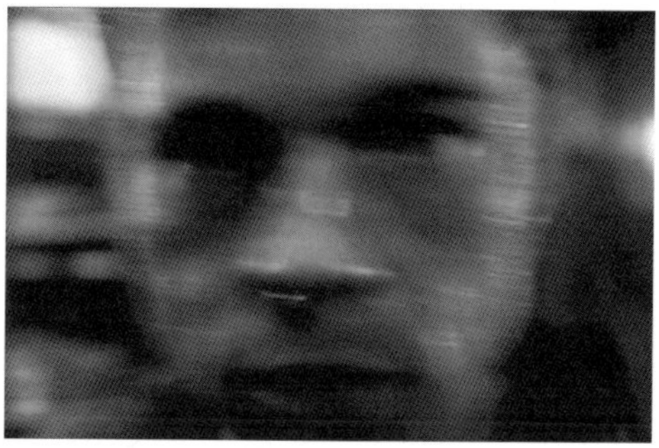

Fight Club, David Fincher, 1999 (Tyler Durden, played by Brad Pitt) - Contaminated image.

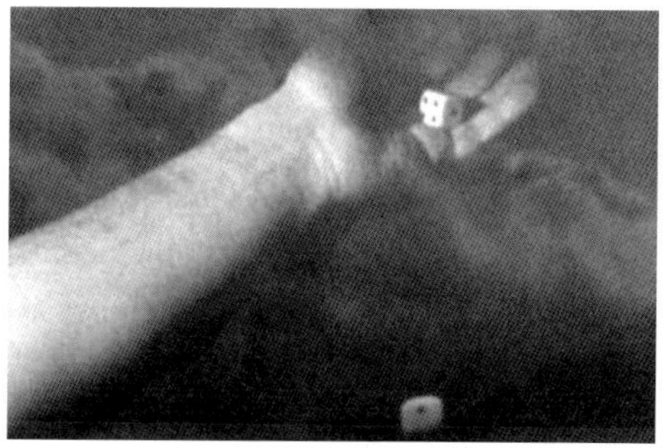

Le jeu de l'oie, Raoul Ruiz, 1980
Overlooking the throw of the dice.

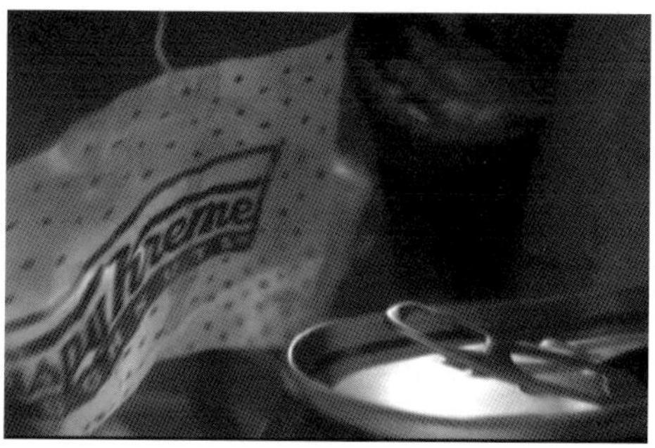

Fight Club, David Fincher, 1999
A camera without a material nature.

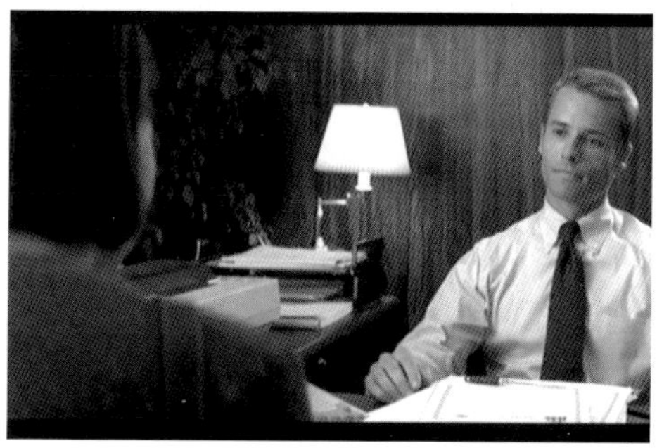

Memento, Christopher Nolan, 2000
(Lenny, played by Guy Pearce)
A meeting that never happened.

ludus-ilinx stated by Perron. Through the excesses of the monstration or the jolts of the narration strictly speaking, those filmic games create vertigo in the spectator by introducing an element of discordance. Without taking into account the simple references to video games, a common stake emerges from the experiments. In Van Sant, Ruiz, Greenaway, there is a will to explore fiction outside the "central conflict", but without resorting to the radical suspension typical of cinematic modernity. The processes we have noted obviously participate in the interpretative sphere developed by each film. An analogy between hermeneutic and game could be considered, which would account among other things for the abstruseness, for the *difficulty* to decode a specific work. Now several processes let us glimpse at an actual confrontation between the narrative level and spectator, concerning narrative comprehension. Our attention will be focused on the spectator's ludic attitude towards the movie.

In the epic narrative, it is usual to approach the imaginary universe a few steps from the ending, *in media res*, at that precise moment which will become the time of the narration, concealed and eventually reached by the explanatory account of the protagonist. That "achronic" device has been fairly usual in cinema over the years; the complete reversal of the chronology, on the opposite, is a relatively recent experience. Ricœur associates the reversal of time with the recollection produced by a second reading (1983: 105). It is precisely through the act of re-narrating, whose charge is assumed by several second narrators in *Citizen Kane* (1941), that Orson Welles already mistreated chronological progression. But at the heart of recent examples like *Memento* (Christopher Nolan, 2000), *Irreversible* (Gaspar Noé, 2002) and *5x2* (François Ozon, 2004), the backwards progression of the scenes/sequences cannot be attributed to any diegetic narrator; it is the plot orchestrator who assumes directly the responsibility for the plot. The status and the effects of the process are obviously a consequence of the frequency of the leaps backwards. In *5x2* and *Irreversible*, one could still talk about "serial flashbacks"; all things considered, the process is no more destabilizing than a classic change of scene, especially since the narrative is still involved in the same nucleus (Marion and Gilles in *5x2*, Alex, Marcus and Pierre in *Irreversible*). At best, the novelty of the process will direct the act of watching towards the *ilinx*, even though the latter will probably compromise with the new rule during the projection. In *Memento*, on the opposite, it becomes extremely difficult to define the progression from one scene to the next in terms of analepses and prolepses, in so far as the original narrative, which opens with Teddy's murder by the protagonist (Lenny), moves back towards an initial point, which is at the same time the starting point of the black and white scenes, interspersed in a systematic way with the original narrative and which actually move forward in time. The frequency of the jumps back in time contributes here to the "mise en phase"[9] of the spectator and the protagonist, without reducing the process to the condition of the latter (short-term memory lapse). By constantly destabilizing the audience, the process lies at the boundaries between *ilinx* and *agon*; it stuns in order to better slow down the comprehension of the universe narrated.

It is well-documented that the double cinematic narrative (level responsible for the first audiovisual narrative/second verbal narrators) often causes some discordances concerning the point of view (cf Gaudreault and Jost, 1990: 45-48). Beyond the primary identification with the camera and in spite of the traditionally desirable self-effacement of the narrative level, the acknowledgement of that level by the spectator is well-established in cinematographic theory. However, discordances on the point of view in contemporary cinema imply a more ambiguous relationship between the spectator and the plot orchestrator. Through the multiplication of red herrings and other cheating trickeries, the relationship between the two poles is more than ever today characterized by antagonization. Thanks to the trend of the "*film à clef*" we can observe in an exemplary way the various modalities of this confrontation. The relevant cases are abundant: *Jacob's Ladder* (Adrian Lynne, 1990), *The Sixth Sense* (M. Night Shayamalan, 1999) *Fight Club* (David Fincher, 1999), *Memento*, *Birth* (Jonathan Glazer, 2004), *El Maquinista* (Brad Anderson, 2004), etc. Before the actual confrontation, the paratextual, and especially the metatextual device, often prepare the spectator to be fooled; several reviews of *The Sixth Sense*, without giving it away, have strongly insisted on the striking nature of the ultimate turn of events. That ultimate sudden change of situation, concerning the narrative, is invariably characterized by an explanatory segment, which provides us with missing information (the key (*clef*)). In the past, the plot orchestrator did justify the omission of key-details by focusing the narration on the protagonist and (the limits of) his knowledge, a common process from Alfred Hitchcock's *Vertigo* (1958), to Robert Schwentke's *Flight Plan* (2005). More recent plots however resort to the complete subjectivisation of the original narrative; the presumption of truth, clinging to the cinematic image and still in force when Hitchcock introduces his famous false flash-back in *Stage Fright* (1950), no longer holds today. In *Memento*, Sammy's story, jointly told by the protagonist and the image only correspond, in the end, to the fabrications of that protagonist

[9] This notion developed by Roger Odin refers to the equation of the relations visible in the fictional world and that of the spectator with the movie.

(visual p.99). The narrator in *Fight Club* and Tyler Durden are both presented in the same shot, lit by the same light, but constitute however a unique person. Besides, Fincher's film makes the "deceptive image" a central case of interest, as can be seen in the shot when the projection seems to collapse (visual p.99), or the altogether improbable flights of the narrator when he fights his imaginary alter ego, nearly impossible yet presented through surveillance cameras. In *The Sixth Sense*, the explanatory keys would like to circumvent such obvious tricks and lies: Doctor Crowe is nothing but another ghost, who wanders "seeing what he wants to see", without being aware of his condition. The omission is thus minimally justified by the character's condition. On the contrary, it becomes highly improbable that the young Cole never witnesses one of those revelatory moments that the lost soul automatically evacuates, that he has never talked about Doctor Crowe with his mother, that he never noticed the doctor's wound, etc. Even though the scenes where the doctor talks alone, in front of his wife, can be justified narratively, they are part of a constant reinforcing that point the spectator in a precise direction, at the risk of coherence.

The radical manipulations of point of view and other processes that we have connected to the *film à clef* directly refer to the work of the plot orchestrator. Through this trend, the spectator is explicitly urged to question the *assumption of truth* evoked by Gaudreault and Jost (1990: 48). The antagonization of the narrating level implies a clever spectator, attentive to clues, busy unraveling the mystery. Obviously that competition is submitted to the promise of a meaning, which prompts some spectators to let themselves be led astray right up to the final revelation. Now what happens if the narrative level never consents to give the keys to its machinations? In *Lost Highway* and *Mulholland Drive* (David Lynch, 1997 and 2001, respectively), the plot orchestrator operates through a throw of the die that redistributes the links between an ensemble of fictive elements. That throw of the die is not a finality in itself but becomes the pivot of the mystery elaborated in each film. From each side of the cut, the scenes echo each other: the aspirations, fears, desires of one character have repercussions in the existence of somebody else. Confronted with numerous symbols, incongruous elements and how many other traps, it is quite unlikely that the spectator will successfully sort out the scenes according to a unique point of view and one precise level of reality. In both cases, that refusal of a closure is immediately conveyed by the last moments of the film, which echo the beginning. In spite of a coefficient of discordance rarely seen since modern experimentations, Lynch tries to involve the spectator in a ludic way. As Ricœur specifies:

> For the work to still catch the reader's interest, the dissolution of the plot must be understood as a signal addressed to the reader to co-operate with the work, to build the plot himself. (...) For that it is necessary of course that the composition by the reader is not made impossible. For the game of waiting, deception and the work of putting things into order again only remains feasible if the conditions of its success are incorporated in the tacit or explicit agreement the author concludes with the reader: I undo the work and you re-do it again—the best you can. (1984:42-43)

At the end of this brief glance at some narrative processes, contemporary popular cinema really seems to integrate more aggressively some discordances. As new strategies are assimilated by the network of the spectator's expectations, those discordances no longer work towards creating a distance for reflection nor a sudden awareness of various perceptive alienations. Considering that, it is hardly surprising that they very often merely reflect the new experiences of fiction associated with video games. As Gardies announced, the new ludic relation with the film lies in its the auto-referentiality, but the meaning of that reflexivity could be reduced to an injunction addressed to the spectator by the film: "play me". "It is true that in that experimentation, the game can become the stake itself" (Ricœur, 1984: 120). Even if the experimentations that we studied —episodic repetition, paradigmatic laying out, reversal of chronology, subjectivisation of the image— were not eventually re-absorbed by concordance, even if the work did refuse to radiate a certain impression of completion, one could bet that the spectator, under the influence of the ludic, would put up with the experience under the modality of vertigo or competition.

*The author wants to thank Richard Bégin and Philippe Mathieu for their support and suggestions.

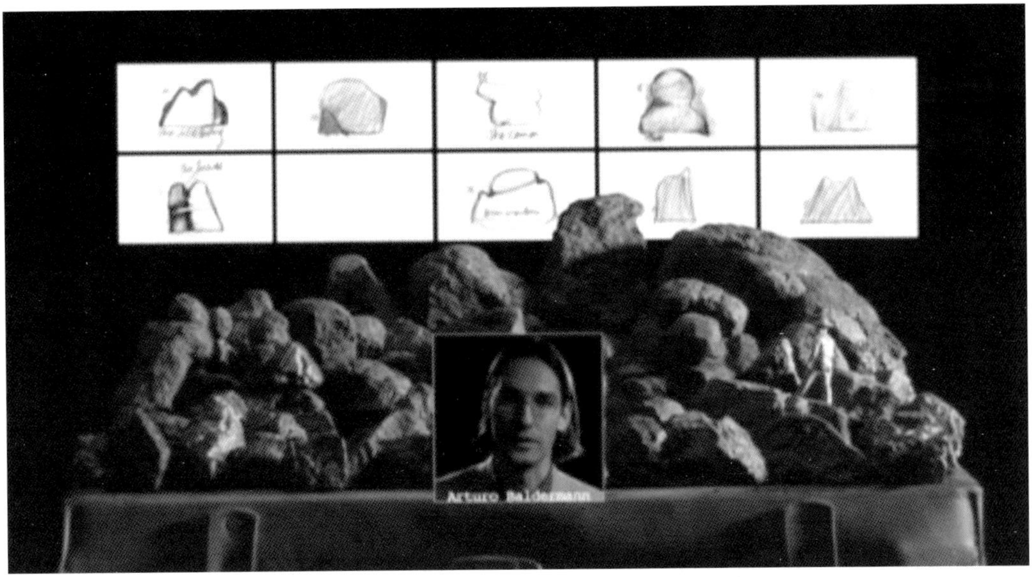

The Tulse Luper Suitcases, Part 1 : The Moab Story de Peter Greenaway, 2003 (Arthuro Balderman, played by Phil Rowlands). Suitcase #1: charcoal bits.

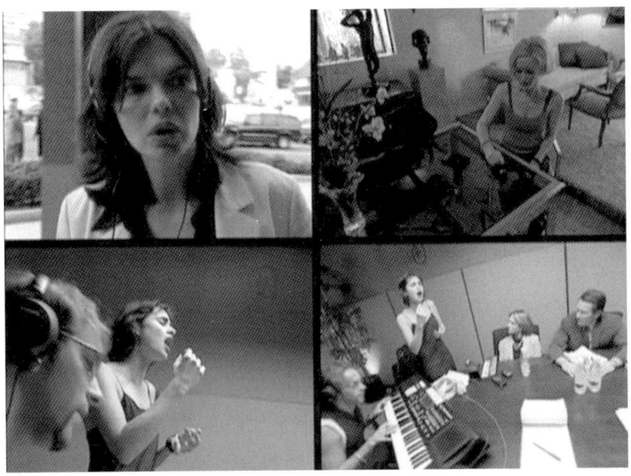

Time Code, Mike Figgis, 2000 - A paradigmatic lay-out.

NARRATION DEAD—STOP. NARRATIVE FOLLOWS

The twentieth century has seen the narrative perish at least twice. The first killing, modern aesthetics, by attracting attention to the substance of the work itself, against the anecdote, treated the lovers of narration like consumers of an illusion or a second-rate artistic production. The formulae used to look down on them were plentiful. As early as 1895, Mallarmé declared that "to narrate, to teach, even to describe, is alright and would probably still be sufficient for most to share human thought," but that those acts of language are part of a "universal documentary" foreign to the "essential" use of speech.[1] Maurice Denis explained "that a painting—before being a battle horse, a naked woman or any anecdote—is essentially a flat surface covered in colors assembled in a certain way,"[2] and Ricardou read into the *nouveau roman* "no longer the writing of an adventure, but the adventure of a writing."[3] Post-modernism, the second killing, at the end of the century, was partly built on the diagnosis of failure of the teleological "great narratives,"—an idea put forward by Jean-François Lyotard—and on its variations, announcing the end of History as a structuring model. That double assertion of lapsing legitimizes questioning the actual forms of narrativity—the conditions that allow any object to shape itself as a narrative, while the second would be the object of our suspicion. But the statement also prompts to slightly shift the question, to follow two axes. On the one hand, to deny narrativity requests to think it as a virtuality, to reflect on a form of availability to the narrative which will be called here *narratability*, and to wonder therefore how to instill narrative where it has been evicted or should not appear. On the other hand, the volatilization of the

[1] Stéphane Mallarmé, "Crise de vers" (1895), *Divagations*, in B. Marchal éd., *Œuvres complètes*, t. II, Paris, Gallimard, Bibliothèque de la Pléiade, 2003, p. 212.

[2] Maurice Denis, cit. in Jean Clay, *L'Impressionnisme*, Hachette, 1971, p. 148.

[3] Jean Ricardou, *Problèmes du nouveau roman*, Paris, Seuil, 1967, p. 111.

unifying "great narratives" allows us to contemplate, for the narration, a form of dispersive survival—or better still, to consider that disintegration as one of the privileged modes of contemporary narrativity. We will see, then, that the entombment of the narrative, far from relegating it off-field (*hors champ*), has undoubtedly contributed to widen its extension, until it has become the equivalent of the field (*champ*), while narrativity was submitted to a series of metamorphoses, a few examples of which will be explored here.

NARRATABILITY AND AUTOREFERENCE

In a formula like Maurice Denis', a certain conception of the reception is in competition with an aesthetic sensitivity not so much new as reserved for a long time for the experts. Facing narrative painting, the model that such a judgement damages assumed that the public, confronted by an ensemble of signs, tells itself a narrative, represented by the work through one of its key-moments (whether it be a battle, an episode, religious or mythical, or merely a family scene like those that Diderot, in his *Salons*, offered to read in Greuze's paintings. The destabilization of that practice of reception was reported by Valéry who, in a passage in his *Cahiers*, linked that transformation to a denarrativisation of the pictorial or poetic subject:

In the nineteenth century, expression and imagination disappear from painting. Everyone who has some talent turns to *still life* (...). Towards 1850, poetry loses subjects in action, the "scenes". (...) One ends up enjoying the *making* itself, the sensation of the *hand* which, in other times, it was essential to make imperceptible. The act of the author takes on proper value. The "drama" shifts. One cannot not see a comedy or falsification in the composition and the expressions of a scenario, and one places the real interest in what only depends upon the eye and the hand, and not credulity, naivety of believing-living.—*That is what I experienced, as far as the story is concerned, quite strongly.*[4]

It is obvious that this crisis of fiction, of "action" and that shifting of the "drama" have, as a result, not a disappearance of the whole story, but the promotion of a genealogy of the work itself: apprehended as a result representing a process, it becomes likely to be read as *the synecdoche of its genesis*. Painting, wrote the poet and critic Bernard Noël, "has become its own subject at the same time as that of the

[4] Paul Valéry, *Cahiers* [1941-1942], Paris, CNRS, 1960, t. XXV, p. 697 (Valéry specifies in the same note that the rejection of narrative subjects admits, however, some exceptions, such as Wagnerian drama, or cinema).

presence of the painter making it: that creates a kind of new narrative, which appears abstract because it no longer seeks its references outside, in history or nature"—and that autoreferential narrativity justifies the title of "novels" he gives to his essays on art.[5] To recreate the narrative of a making appears as a modality always available to the aesthetic gaze. The most abstract image, the less narrative and paradoxically the less "made", ends up representing, minimally, the succession of actions which have led to its reception as a work of art. In addition, the more disconcerting the work is with regard to the expectation of the public, the more it's likely to attract such a kind of hermeneutic, in so far as every object submitted to a questioning on its purpose tends to become the object of a genealogical narration. So the modern and contemporary creation is not the only one to generate that type of reception. A means to revisit the patrimony, the works of art most strongly associated with a traditional narrative logic are themselves "put into narrative" as sites for manufacturing their own final forms, thanks to the development of techniques of analysis and reconstruction which are used to reveal and publish the processes of trial and error, the corrections and drafts. X rays, for example, in an extension of the visible proposal to visitors, reveal beneath the surface of classic paintings alternative versions, or second thoughts, as new archeological strata offered to the attention of the public in museums. Even more precisely, concerning texts, a particular theoretical school, the genetic critique, has been working for some thirty years in gathering and putting in order the various remains of works of art, from the first sketch to the last corrected proofs, in fields as diverse as literature, music, sciences, even architecture, in order to apprehend the creative gesture as a "*making*, an activity, a movement," and "networks of operations"[6] to reconstruct and analyze.

By coming into general use, the position which consists in observing the artistic composition as the vestige of a series of creative events and structural decisions spread over time, tends to give back to the objects a particular plasticity, by exploiting, whether their content is or not a narrative, a narratability linked to that story itself. Far from starting up a withdrawal of the narrative, it has led instead to multiplying its levels of application: every work of art narrates its fabrication and thus, its possibles. Therefore, Valéry's reflection takes on considerable scope. Linking an attempt at denarrativisation of the aesthetic subjects to the emergence of an increased attention to the making, he shows that man never escapes narrativity.

[5] Bernard Noël, *Romans d'un regard*, Paris, POL, 2003, p. 133. For a more detailed analysis of that designation, see Hugues Marchal, "L'examen des titres: les 'romans' critiques de Bernard Noël", in D. Vaugeois dir., *L'Écrit sur l'art: un genre littéraire?, Figures de l'art* n°9, 2005, p. 181-193.

[6] Almuth Grésillon, *Eléments de critique génétique: lire les manuscrits modernes*, Paris, PUF, 1994, p. 7 and 15.

Far from resulting in the expected eviction of the fable, the aesthetic position he describes comes under that "indicial paradigm" of which Carlo Ginzburg has shown the significance in the formation of the clinical, historiographical or police disciplines at the end of the nineteenth century.[7] The modern public will have thus reconnected with the reading the ancestral hunter used to subject the tracks of the animals to, in order to deduce information on their path (a reading which would be, it seems, at the origin of writing). If to interpret is to narrate (to oneself) the work, that work is well and truly received as part of a narrative practice, even though strictly speaking it doesn't present *any* of the criteria for narrativity, defined by Gerald Prince as "the set of properties characterizing narratives and distinguishing them from non-narratives."[8] And the stake has to move towards discourses of accompaniment which constitute the work in auto-narration.

That transformation of the reception obviously had consequences in the creation itself, the two poles influencing each other. In literature, Francis Ponge's approach, when he published the whole of the preliminary texts of some of his poems, is exemplary to that evolution. In *La Fabrique du pré* and *Comment une figue de paroles et pourquoi*, two books which respectively offer the file of "Le Pré" and "La figue (sèche)", the reader discovers, not a series of different poems, but the evolution of the writing towards one single final poem. His crossings-out and additions become the events to read and chronologically identify, so that a non-narrative work, belonging to what Valéry called "still life" (meaning here, the description of the differential qualities of the meadow (le pré) or the fig (la figue)) becomes well and truly the narrative of its own putting-into-work, or into variation. On the same level, the novelist François Bon, who had already agreed for an exhibition on "writers' drafts" to write a text on the computer while retaining a particular program registering his corrections, so as to let the visitors read on the screen the work in progress, in a kind of animation where the words were put together or erased, offers today on his site some documents on the drafts of his writings: "from now on," he explains, "the Internet image of the workshop of a book, with iconography, complementary material, studies and links, is progressively formed, as soon as the first sentences are written."[9] Doubling up the

[7] Cf. Carlo Ginzburg, *Clues, Myths, and the Historical Method*, Baltimore, The Johns Hopkins University Press, 1989.

[8] Gerald Prince, "Narrativity", in D. Herman et al., *Routledge encyclopedia of narrative theory*, Routledge, London-New York, 2005, p. 387.

[9] http://www.tierslivre.net/arch/index.html#livres.

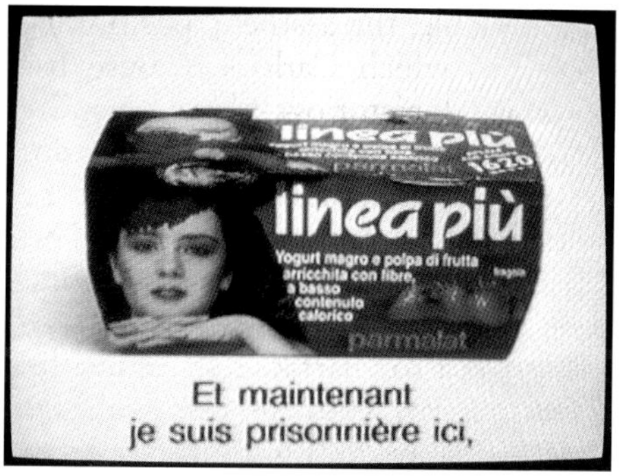

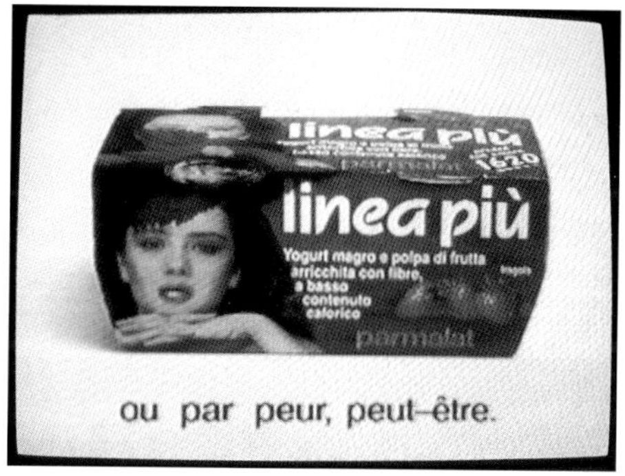

Withering I (details), Guillaume Paris, 1998, video (with Daniela Attanasio).

Il n'est plus question du personnage

⇒ ils ne voient plus **C. Tramell.** [*I.e.* l'apparition délibérée/dans le scénario de son sexe a, chez certains (nombreux), pour conséquence qu'il n'est plus question du personnage : l'espace de trois secondes, le film est perçu comme un reportage sur **Sharon Stone**.]

12h : C'est donc un second coup de poignard. **Ducruet** devrait perdre en quelques semaines tous les avantages acquis par son mariage : adieu princesse, bonjour tristesse.
Le destin de **Steph** a pris un tournant irrévocable : elle en a trop vu

Elle en a trop vu pour pouvoir encore supporter

c'est l'instant incontournable.
Dimanche 15 septembre :
Et c'est encore les derniers rayons de soleil
13h : Comme tous les **dimanches**, les derniers rayons de l'été : **Steph** en profite et redevient la **maman courage**.
15h05 : Elle expose son visage aux rayons. Pour leur montrer à tous
à tous, à eux, qu'elle n'est pas que la femme bafouée : elle fait front. Le temps passe à une vitesse folle et elle commence à s'y faire.
21h15 : Il passe des soirées entières sans elle, il ne

Fini le temps où le couple descendait fièrement les marches du palais…

tendresse…
du **Replay Store** la boutique où il lui arrive de tenir parfois elle-même la caisse
ou **23h30** accoudé à la table du **Jimmy's**, la boîte branchée de Monaco, **DD** vide verre sur verre. Il se sait pris au piège.

NB : XXXVI
LE DÉSIR DE PEINDRE

<u>**Notule**</u>

M. S*** fabrique, avec quelques complices, des *événements réels* (accouplements, accidents, adultères, divorces et même conflits, guerres, etc.) dans le seul but de les photographier et de les revendre aux revues les plus offrantes, qui pourront, dès lors, publier le mélange photos + texte qu'on connaît.

Petits poëmes en prose, Christophe Hanna, Al Dante, Paris 1998, p. 40.

completed and printed text, the site, equal to the files published by Ponge, offers elements of its genesis. Now such devices, like the critical discourses which support them, encourage the receptor to reconstitute, beyond the narrativity effectively programmed by the final work, the narrative of a text-making (itself eventually fictionalisable by the authors). They request therefore above all what Viviane Asselin calls a "narrative reading", meaning a *voluntary position of reception* at the end of which the "non-narrative can be read narratively", opening up to a definition of narrativity "which appears then indissociable from the interpretative decisions a reader implements through the course of the text."[10] Reciprocally, any singular work of art, conceived as a stage, can present itself as a provisional state in a work that is assimilated to the very existence of its creator. It is for example the limit experience led by Orlan, whose photographs *document* an undertaking of surgical modification of the body of the artist, spread over several years. The whole production offers itself as a narrative polyptic *in progress*, which relates the story of its own constitution as an open series.

If that point is relatively well-known, less studied has been the way which, another means to constitute themselves as an event, some works take as subject not only their creation, but also their consumption, seized, in its turn, as a temporal chain. *A Suitable Boy* by the Indian writer Vikram Seth (1993), a vast family saga recounting the beginning of contemporary India, includes the character of a writer who speaks ironically about the mode of reception of long novels, on which he theorizes two methods of possible reading: either one would abandon it after reading a large number of pages, or, on the contrary, one would dive into it to the detriment of one's social life. Now the humoristic impact of such a passage is due to the way it overflows the narrative told, to comment the narrative read, calling for the audience to be aware of its own workings, that is, according to Umberto Eco's phrase, of the position, both external and *in fabula*, of the *lector*. In the same way, in *Dans ces bras-là*, Camille Laurens presents a series of portraits of men, which ends on an unexpected address to the "recipient", a chapter in which the novelist explains to her audience that she needs to think of it as male, looking for an answer from that reader, while knowing that she won't get any. "I shall never be in your arms", she notes, before adding, the final sentence of the text, that she dreams of such an encounter, to end up "in those arms! (dans ces bras-là!)" Through a strange collapse of the barrier between narrative and reality, the male recipient is suddenly included in the story, since he is specifically holding the book

[10] Viviane Asselin, "S'acquitter de la convention narrative: le lecteur floué par le récit", in C. Deltombe and A. Marchand dir., *Le lecteur, enjeu de fiction, Cahiers du CERACC*, n° 3, june 2006 <www.ecritures-modernite.cnrs.fr/roman_cahiers3.html>.

"in his arms", at the moment the novelist expresses that wish. The gesture of reading becomes, outside the text, the last event, continually repeatable and reproduced, of that autobiographic book, and it is thus its encounter with the text itself which becomes the substance for a fictional narrative—that of a carnal union truly phantasmatic.[11] In those two examples the narrative tends to go beyond its usual limits. It becomes including, inclusive, even intrusive: the reader ends up discovering, in what he reads, the description of the continuation of his own acts and he attends his own work as actor of the creation as a temporal and cognitive unfolding. It is therefore the trial of an uncanny, injunctive narratability that he is induced to literally live, since he sees his acts obeying the indications which seem written in advance by the text, confusing the temporal compartimentations and the separation between fictive and real.[12]

CONTRACTS AND COUNTER-INVESTIGATIONS: THE PRODUCT AS NARRATOR AND AS FABLE(S)

Such an injunctive method is found, on another level altogether, in most of the advertising devices, which function as promises. From the very first advertising, the consumer of goods and services has changed into a buyer of prophetic narratives, in the sense that he is deemed to acquire, through the promoted product, a series of actions both desirable and to come, whose subject and beneficiary he will be. In the past, a famous campaign in France offered an obvious example of that teleological structure, by praising a car for the male audience thanks to the slogan, albeit lacking subtlety: "He has the car, he will have the girl". The correlation between the gesture of acquiring the car and the appearance of a second event, constituent of the putting into place of a narrative dynamics, is enunciated very clearly in that formula. The before/after sequence, so typical of advertising strategies, reproduces the most fundamental logic of the narrative as the passage from one state to another. Between them, the buying of the object designates the latter as the pivot and thus the material equivalent of the narrative. The audience

[11] Camille Laurens, *Dans ces bras-là*, Paris, POL, 2000, p. 296-297.

[12] Those literary games are to be compared to the way Bernard Noël, like other critics, ends up, on the same basis, defining the pictorial experience not only as the reconstruction of an archeology, but also as the simultaneous consuming by the spectator of his own looking activity, another subject for a narrative. If "in all constructions, even the most abstract, (there are) traces of a narrative that the eyes perceive and take note of" (*op.cit.* p. 111), he explains, "because of the ambiguity which is always established between the visible and the act of seeing, you no longer distinguish the movement of your feelings from the movement that the painting seems to give them. In reality any mobility is in your eyes, and it is that alone which makes the painting move" (p.131), so that "the painting makes (...) coexist in its confined space, layers of time, which each corresponds to a different present" (p.143).

must consider the acquired goods or service as the beginning, or at least the catalyst, for the following events, and we are all, in that respect, Perrette with a pail of milk (*organic* and *light*, that goes without saying), since we see in each "object of desire" the *incipit* of a dreamt autobiography. Even when the purchase allows us to get a *standing*—meaning a past as much imagined as the offered future, that status acquired with the object is the opposite of a *status quo*: it has to be useful for an evolution. It makes emblematic an individual plan of participation in a collective narration; in other words it allows the consumer, appropriating the narrative structure of the object, to assume its promising story.

The narrowing of the formats and the increased competition for the public attention have led to increasingly superimpose promise and product, so as to intensify the metonymic and connotative relation which unites them: the advertising narrative is made to be more and more minimalist and allusive. If the commodities on display concentrate something, it's therefore first of all the trajectory of life of which they present themselves as a portion and as a guarantee—by materializing it. In that sense, the consumer's goods can appear *par excellence*, in themselves, as *summaries of narrative*, or rather, *narratives.*

The plural imposes itself for, typically, the vestigial approach still works here. In each consumer's goods, the two types of potential narration cross path intimately. The narratability of the phantasmatic and euphoriant promise begins with the product, creates a desire and tells a future in which the consumer projects himself as a hero, for it offers to measure the value of the product to the use he will make of it. It readily provokes in the writers, a counter-narrative that at the same time actualizes and questions the proposed thread. So, in a documentary written in 1996 for *Harpers' Magazine*, "A Supposedly Fun Thing I'll Never Do Again," David Foster Wallace exploits that dimension by confronting the account of his cruise on a luxury liner with the scenario offered in the advertising leaflet, a promise "that one will succeed—at least, for once—to relax completely and to enjoy oneself, because one won't have the *choice* not to enjoy oneself,"[13] which increasingly pulls up short as the text progresses. The other type of narration, that of manufacturing, realist and of Marxist origin, joins the aesthetics of the making. It ends with the product, for it tells its actual genesis and its conditions of manufacturing. Its main elements appear, in a minimal form, on most of the manufactured products since the 1930 American *Tariff act,* which led to the general use of the words "made in"—a form of indication in increased development as the principle of the traceability of the goods has imposed itself, which ensures that each

[13] "A Supposedly Fun Thing I'll Never Do Again," in *A Supposedly Fun Thing I'll Never Do Again* (1997), Boston, Little, Brown & Co.

consumer can reconstruct the story of the product. The narrations which give it a try, readily take on the form of an investigation: their driving force is suspicion and they therefore tend to make of the object, the piece of evidence of a crime—a phenomenon noticed and used by Naomi Klein in her essay *No Logo*: "the considerable attention of investigative journalists for the places of anonymous origin of the highly identified goods", which has led, among other things, "to retrace the journey of the Nike sport shoes to the Vietnamese sweat shops; and of the Barbie accessories to Sumatra's child labor."[14] Around the objects, the two narrative unfoldings compete with each other, the dysphoric reality of the conditions of manufacturing or real use often invalidating the advertising promise.

There, where the Balzacian narrator used to describe the possessions of the heroes to provide the reader with so many clues on the trajectory of the protagonists, the accessories of the contemporary subject offer him a library of economic stories and personal dreams, between which he chooses and with which he plays like a repertoire. That role has been underlined by Brett Easton Ellis in *American Psycho* (1991). That novel never ceases to enumerate the luxury brands of the clothes worn by the characters, the theoretical guarantees of desirable heroic qualities, but in reality, functioning like so many lures contrasting with the sadistic behavior of the hero, while multiplying, through the accumulation of those references, a kind of interruption of the plot by some advertising references, which mimic at the same time the experience of contemporary consumption of any long narration (especially on TV) and the inclusion of references to brands whose firms pay the production for those inserts (especially in cinema, where the script writers take those writing constraints into account). In the field of visual arts, in much the same way, that kind of narratability has been explored and adapted with irony by several artists. Guillaume Paris, for example, treats consumer goods like "beings-made-into-things", whose value as fetish he questions, as well as their links with a form of *magical* efficiency. His videos stage those objects by giving life to the models which appear on the wrappers, and by putting into their mouths an autobiographical discourse which actualizes the equivalence between goods and narration: making the product-portrait speak intensifies the structural logic of the merchandise and helps to "find again a subjectivity and thus, to re-inject a story, a biography, an actual experience." But the statement put into their mouth by Paris comes into conflict with the dynamics promised by the advertising logic, to emphasize the character atemporal, meaning truly *ecstatic,* of that promise: the wrappers carry the marks of rotting, the narrative of the models evokes a locking-up, and an editing in loop expresses a harking-back, so that the "transitory nature

[14] Naomi Klein, *No logo.* London, Flamingo, 2001 p. 20.

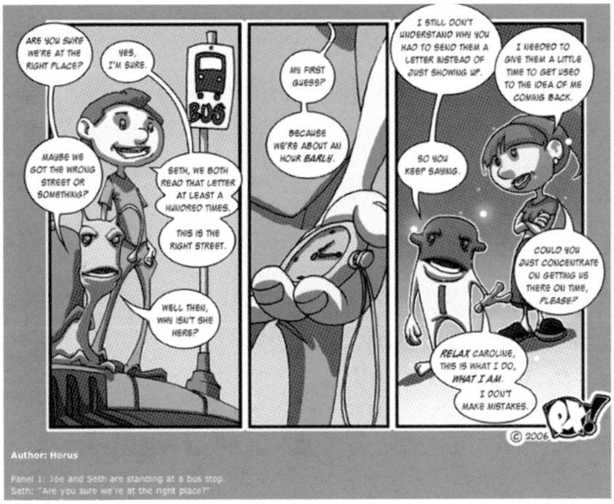

PandaXpress, taken from the screen of the forum site from january 16 2006, changed according to an evolution in the script proposed by a visitor
(<http://www.pandaxpress.com/forum/viewtopic.php?p=1684>).

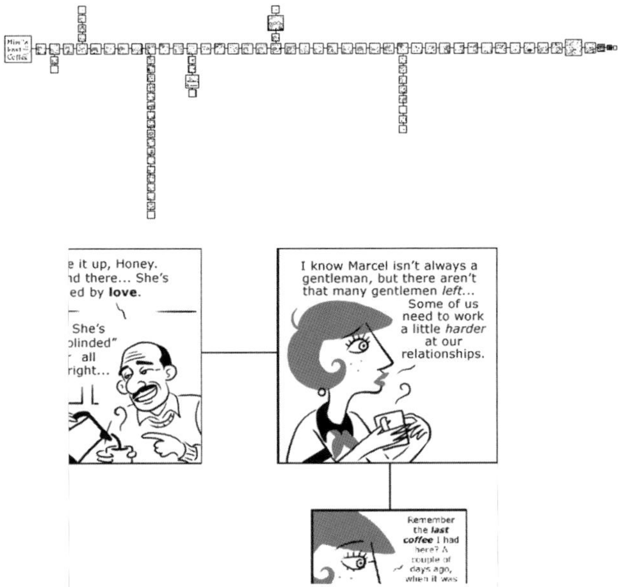

Mimi's last coffee, Scott McCloud, 2004, overall view and details from the web comic organized like an arborescence with multiple endings.
(<http://www.scottmccloud.com/comics/mi/mi-26/mi-26.html>).

of things and beings is put forward", to "inject inside the representation itself the germ of its own destruction."[15]

The actualization of narratability of the objects in the works of creation becomes, as we can see, strongly critical, in the double sense of an explanation and a questioning of its functioning. They underline to what extent the complex potential narrativity, embodied in the objects and linked to their circulation, transform our whole environment in a fabric saturated with narratives or embryos of narratives, in which the biography of goods and that of the characters are mixed. The variations to which they submit some of those narrative objects divert their discourses and describe the possibility of a game with that prolix system of fables.

FROM BODY-INFORMATION TO POSTHUMAN NARRATIONS

That putting into narration equally touches the living, under the influence of biology, which urges associating genetic code, organic messages and linguistic texts. We witness then an extension to the human actors of the logic of traceability: the social agents become their own autobiography. If our financial dealings, our communications or our moves even, are already recorded in a kind of doubling up agenda, allowing an authorized or non-authorized third person to reconstitute our story (a phenomenon widely treated in investigative or spy narratives), nothing prevents us from imagining a future in which the practices of biometry will make at any time our interlocutors capable of having at their disposal not only a face and a moment, but also a comparable chronological account accompanying the meeting of an exchange of retrospective data which will always limit the possibilities for any of us to escape our past. That potential fusion between the present of an organic and social subject, and its narrative (or its fiction) of life, is a theme exploited in *Cosmos Incorporated*, by Maurice G. Dantec. The contract killer who, at the beginning of that science fiction novel, goes through the customs identity control without any problem, can logically be dealt with like this: "We, he, you, I, whatever, his personality is factitious. His eye print is factitious, a good part of his body is factitious (…). A good part of his existence, consequently, is factitious."[16] However, such a situation is more widely typical of *cyberpunk*, which Dantec can be linked to. In reality, that literary movement associates a work of formal mutation of the narrative models with a reflection on the future of a human species

[15] Guillaume Paris, *Mixed blessings*, dir. Cécile Dazord, Musée d'art moderne et contemporain de Strasbourg, 2002, p. 104-105.

[16] Maurice G. Dantec, *Cosmos incorporated*, Paris, Albin Michel, 2005, p. 17.

for a long time considered as a historical invariant, but given back to time with the theories of evolution which have been feeding for a century now, a "great narrative" at the same time genealogical and prospective which hasn't stopped gaining an audience. Now cyberpunk insists on the new links between body and texts that science brought to light, and crosses that approach with the rise of the information technologies, in order to make permeable the limits between living, subject and narration.[17] Its writers break new grounds in so far as they tackle the ontology of the text, of the narrator or receptor, following paradigms and questioning coming from the new biology, so that in their most successful creations, the science fiction plot becomes the way to experiment on the foundations of fiction. That union has been expressed directly in the title of the founding novel of that movement, which makes of William Gibson's *Neuromancer* (1984) the work of a *neuro mancer*, but also a *new romancer*. The correlation is shown in one of the themes privileged by those texts: one witnesses not the end of the narrative, but the multiplication of the narrative of the end of the human for the benefit of the birth of a kind of "post-human" narration.

In *Blood Music,* Greg Bear imagines a manipulation that would make each of our cells intelligent. He builds a novel whose human protagonists end up being perceived as individuals, as agglomerates of those thinking cells or "noocytes", and as mere parts of the whole consciousness which form the ensemble of the living bodies, gathered in a mass endowed with all the singular biographies and with the memory of its own apparition. Here is an example of the way such an experience of thought modifies narration and language: one of the characters, Bernard, ends up visiting his own body in the form of an aggregate of cells, experiencing (in himself) the existence of a multitude of subjects both divergent and identical to his own identity, with the result that several variants of the "self" bear witness to his experience. And the humans then receive personal and foreign words coming from that mutant body, marked with otherness by a sign indicating the inadequate quality of some terms in relation to the narrative that the cells try to relate in sequences like "WORDS communicate with •share body structure external• is this like •wholeness WITHIN• •totality• is EXTERNAL alike."[18] Beyond the logical tensions and the efforts on the willing suspension of disbelief the fiction demands from its reader, Bear transposes in a narrative the identity vacillation orchestrated by contemporary biology. His novel, as a deconstruction of the subject, a blend of

[17] Cf. Larry McCaffery, *Storming the Reality Studio: A Casebook of Cyberpunk and Postmodern Science-Fiction*, Durham, Duke University Press, 1991.

[18] Greg Bear, *Blood Music* [1985], London, Gollancz, coll. SF Masterworks, 2001, p. 83.

voice and discourse and an articulation of ill-assorted fictional compartments (several characters living that metamorphosis differently, and several biological levels of the "self" telling, for some of those players, the same experience), illustrates and narratively exploits the questioning generated by the scientific representations. In *Cosmos Incorporated*, the character of the killer, whose account almost permanently adopts his own viewpoint, appears like a *clean slate*, a pure surface with no memory. In the first pages, he merely records his movements, when he goes through customs without difficulty, while appearing to himself discover the information answering the questions he is asked, among them his own name, Plotkine. But hour after hour, aboard a train whose progression is used as a metaphor for the progression of the reading itself, he recovers a hidden memory in some of his cells, and therefore, his identity and his mission: to shoot down a target. Here too, because the biologic vulgate allows the association of genetic code and linguistic archive, the character finds himself in a particular position: Plotkine only discovers himself as his narration, in real time, progresses, so that he is both narrator in the strict sense—he describes for example the landscape he sees from the train, or the organic modifications which happen inside him—and narratee of the memories he gradually reveals, as well as the task he has to accomplish.

> During the course of the journey, all his memory implants, having until now remained scrupulously inactive, will release their stocks of information, completing the shaping of the Man come to kill another man.[19]

So that when "the signal to open the still inactive last cells" operates,

> It is a whole narrative that finally takes shape.
> It is a whole story that is woven in his own hands, in the quicksilver fire of the electric light and the high speed (of the train).[20]

With such an opening, the author can move the classic stakes of the launching of the plot, taken in charge here by the "neuron implants", while the character is compared to a white page, on which a curious allo/autobiography is printed, precisely the book the reader is reading. But this initial situation, in which the boundaries between text and narrator are made to be blurred, grows rapidly complex, when the character becomes aware of the irreconcilable character of some

[19] *Cosmos Incorporated*, p. 33.
[20] *Id.*, p. 41.

of the memories that are given back to him. He ceases then to define those (and, consequently, his own past, as well as his "character"), as a factual narrative, to think of himself as fiction:

> So, as the outside world comes to light as a network of concentric waves whose temporary reverberating center he is, the first foundations of his personality appear, tracing the topography particular to that territory, like the strange weaving of a semantic map (...). His personality itself—with the exception of the information delivered to him by the instructions' neurons program—is undoubtedly composed of an audacious and perfectly non-disentangled mix of true and false memories. He is several lives in one, but not one is complete. None is true, none is false either.[21]

The novel is then narrated following the point of view of its own narration—a play on words, written from the very beginning in the character's name, *plot* in its English sense, and *kin* echoing the idea of similarity or identity.[22] Consequently the hero will learn that he has in fact no past, and has only been synthesized for that mission by another character, comparable to an "angel", which will show himself capable of giving life to his own narratives—so that as a narrator, the angel meets his own fictional creation. Now the evolution of the plot will lead that creator to give back his freedom of actions to the character, then to invest him with his own aptitude to make his fictions real, so that, described first as "incarnated fiction", Plotkine is confirmed "metafiction made flesh."[23] At the end of the story he divides in two, to describe from his hotel room the actions he undertakes simultaneously with other characters, changing into the programmer of a fiction which, however, includes him. We are confronted with a confused narrative, whose main player has the triple status of narrated (his journey is told), of narrative text (he is the product of a narration by another character), and of narrator (it is him who rules the events read)—along a game where each stratum creating reality ends up fictionalized by the next.

Other key components of narrativity suffer similar treatment to that which here perturbs the narrator function. Thus, with *Villa Vortex*, the same Dantec has composed a novel whose construction, this time, follows the model of a biological mutation, to materialize during the time of the reading a kind of biological leap whose object would be the text itself. The components of a first narrative fall to pieces to become the object of an uncertain rearrangement in the second part of the

[21] *Id.*, p. 48-49.

[22] The novel delays that evidence until the very last pages, which designate Plotkine as "the man of the *plot*, the man of action" (p. 516).

[23] *Id.*, p. 416.

book—an imitation founded on the assimilation of the generic code itself to a "novel of our biological life, (...) producing around a hundred thousand paragraphs or chapters, each, a gene, coding *the history* of a protein necessary to such or such function in such or such organ."[24] In all cases, borrowing from the biological models implies a preconceptualization of the body as potential narration or narrator, an exchange which underlines the role of *general equivalent* assigned to the narrative—a means to think about the embodied subject as its productions.

Faced with that "whole narrative", a certain form of disappearance of the "great narrative" could simply indicate the sudden awareness of a situation of global competition between the various potential narrative unities which form our environment, but also, if there is an end of History, between the various historical or geographical modes of narrative with, in contemporary works, various logics of dispersal, if not, executions of the discourse which bear witness less to a move back than to an omnipresence of the narrative.

DISPERSED NARRATIVES

To apprehend the field as a mesh of potential narratives amounts to placing ourselves within a myriad of simultaneous narrative propositions, a polyphony that the mediatic sphere is emblematic of, particularly by multiplying the close variations on fictional or actual stories.[25]

It is the typical experience of the modern consumer-citizen to live in the middle of a constant bundle of information and fables that compete to catch his attention and interpenetrate as our journeys of submission to their discourse unfold. The cultural works do not escape those conditions of reception, dominated by hybridizations and interruption, and their deviations facing traditional models of narration can be treated as so many reactions to that framework. The French

[24] Maurice G. Dantec, "La fiction comme laboratoire anthropologique expérimental" (1997), *Périphériques*, Seuil, 2003, p. 132-133. For a study and more detailed history of the use of the split narrators, according to models borrowed from biology, see H. Marchal, "De si petits penseurs: le narrateur, ses cellules, ses microbes", *La Voix du regard*, n° 17, pp. 8-23. And for an analysis of the model of the mutation in *Villa Vortex*, see "Mutation biologique et avant-gardes littéraires", *Critique*, n° 709-710, june-july 2006, p. 566-579.

[25] Marc Lits insists on the appearance of a "dynamics of narrativised mediatisation, or mediatic narrativity" such as "the mediatised information is one of the main places for the structuration of the imagination of contemporary societies (as much if not more than fiction)", and that "that information is transmitted via micro-narratives which we consume and co-construct simultaneously" and, we will add, permanently ("Information, médias et récit médiatique", *Belphégor*, n°1, november 2001, <etc.dal.ca/belphegor/vol1_no1/articles/01_01_Lits_Info_fr.html>).

Christophe Hanna gives, with his *Petits poëmes en prose*, a representation of that. Beneath an ironic title, taken from Baudelaire, he offers a series of collages that create typographically that saturation of concomitant narratives. The reader is faced with a network of narrations interrupting one another, and opening the space of the page to multiple narrative forms deemed non-literary like news items, tabloids or erotic small ads, while here and there some metatextual commentaries appear. A device which is close to that is the *dazibao* shown for a whole night, in 2004, on the Paris university campus of Jussieu by Hou Hanru, who projected on fifteen or so screens placed next to each other, some hundred artists' videos, in a kind of visual cacophony offering an emblem of the general conditions of consumption of that type of sequences.[26] Not only, as in museums and galleries, where the public tries to grasp those art pieces, the process of uncertain division linked to the movements of each spectator made problematic the chronological structuration of those artists' films, which, in essence, are narrative, since they lie on a succession of images, but the parasite action which the sequences mutually inflicted on each other reproduced the way some art works compete with others, artworks which control less and less their environment and their order. Consequently, a general evolution of the narrations occurs towards the double task of capturing the public's attention and taking into account the interruption, which has probably begun with the emergence of the mediatic society, before the year 1850 even, when the appearance of an "industrial literature" was accompanied by the adoption of a *découpage* in episodes, dictated to the long narrative by the demands of prepublication in the daily press. Used as a way to captivate the readership, the narrative series stops on a cliff hanger, imposing on the narrative a structure favoring both interruption and continuity, and supporting the composition of chapters both autonomous and literally perforated by a lack of information aiming at tormenting the reader's curiosity.

Articulating deception and promise, such a model could in reality have paved the way to works of art which, without submitting to the demands of the mass media, have adopted deceptive forms, which give up as lost the unity, by accepting in various degrees those apparent constraints. Some request excess, others on the contrary favor cutting and rarefaction, the two strategies combining with each other.

As examples of the play on excessiveness, in the United States, the nineties were marked by the rise of complex and often long narrative comics, the *graphic novels*, like *Suck rubber baby* by Howard Cruse (1995), and the publication of novels such as Thomas Pynchon's *Mason and Dixon* (1997), or Don DeLillo's

[26] "Nuit blanche", 2 october 2004, Université Pierre et Marie Curie.

marche à suivre pour le port des gilets de sauvetage et de tout un jeu de cartes DO NOT DISTURB suspendues à la poignée intérieure[60]. Le vestibule est large une fois et demie comme moi. La salle de bain est attenante au vestibule d'un côté; de l'autre on trouve le Wondercloset, dédale compliqué d'étagères, tiroirs, cintres, vide-poches et Coffre Personnel à l'Épreuve du Feu. Le Wondercloset tire parti du moindre centimètre cube avec tant d'ingéniosité qu'il n'y a qu'une chose en dire : il doit avoir été conçu par quelqu'un de vraiment très méthodique. À l'opposé de la cabine, une large corniche en émail court tout le long du mur bâbord en dessous d'une fenêtre qu'il convient je crois d'appeler hublot[61]. Comme ceux que l'on voit à la télé, mon hublot est effectivement rond, en revanche il n'est pas petit, et pour traduire le rôle qu'il joue dans l'atmosphère et la raison d'être de la pièce, on peut le comparer à la rosace d'une cathédrale. Il est découpé dans ce verre très épais qui protège les employés de banque. Dans un coin, on lit :

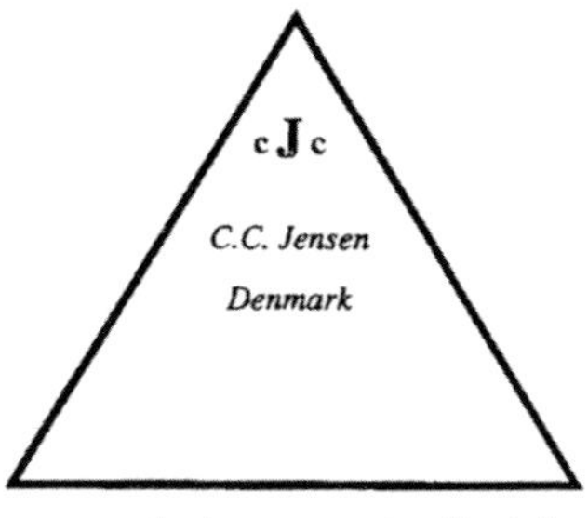

60. L'agoraphobe non anglophone sera réconforté d'apprendre que ce jeu inclut BITTE NICHT STÖREN, PRIÈRE DE NE PAS DÉRANGER, SI PREGA NON DISTURBARE, et (mon préféré de tous) FAVOR DE NO MOLESTAR.

61. Si vous êtes un enfant de moins de douze ans ou un anorexique, vous pouvez probablement vous asseoir sur ce rebord pour contempler rêveusement la mer, mais une bordure externe saillante qui veut du mal à votre postérieur rend la chose impraticable pour un adulte de taille normale.

Un truc soit disant super auquel on ne me reprendra plus (A Supposedly Fun Thing I'll Never Do Again), David Foster Wallace, (French translation éd. Au Diable Vauvert, 2005,p. 476-477 - English version published by Little, Brown & Co, Boston, 1997).

Underworld (1997), whose imposing size meets, as Seth's novel, *A Suitable Boy*, an undeniable desire for totality, linked to a reflection on the historical evolution of the country. That situation, very different from the French-speaking fictional landscape, in which one witnesses a rarefaction of such synthetic narratives, invites us to moderate the failure of the "great narrative," except to admit that this stating, opening onto the postmodern condition, includes the possibility of its remanence. Thus an assemblage of micro-narratives reproducing, at various degrees, the uncertainty generated by the surrounding polyphony (or polemophony) takes over the unifying narration in those texts too.[27] Although already old, the phenomenon remains especially used and associated with a kind of modernity, undoubtedly because of its homology with the variation to which the multiplication of sources and vectors of information submits the phenomena related by the media. A novel like *The Human Stain* by Philip Roth (2000) draws a great part of its effectiveness from the confrontation of several contradictory versions of the hero's story, a Jewish university professor accused of racism towards his Afro-American students, but who will prove to be an Afro-American himself, having concealed his origins since the end of his adolescence. Linked to the use of several points of view, but also to the inclusion of rumors and lies, the successive narratives complete each other, correct each other, and in the end, prevent the main narrator, a novelist, from creating the narrative of that journey: the novel is built like that, declaring its own failure about to happen, as much as the impossibility to choose between fiction and "truth". With a strategy similar to Roth's novel, a text like *Martin and John*, by Dale Peck[28] prevents the story from becoming stable by weaving a narrative frame—in which the narrator, John, reports on various moments of his own life and his relationship with his dead lover, Martin—and a series of short stories written by the same John, but in which the main plot is told with inconsistent variants, only the names of the protagonists remaining identical. The reader follows a narrative which divides into alternative sections, both linked and divergent, presumed to be fictional or presented as factual—creating an uncertainty which invites us to connect its use by Dale Peck to a *queer* aesthetics. And last, some narratives let the reader choose between several possible resolutions. It is, for example, a path explored in comics by Scott McCloud, with *Mimi's last coffee*, a story which presents itself like an arborescence of scenarios simultaneously followed by the author, so that the initial unity gives

[27] On those conflicts between narrative modalities, one should approach the whole of the post-colonial texts, marked by a complex hybridization between allogenic narrative models, but also, again, some of the science-fiction texts which rely upon the staging of narrators having different perceptions of time, like in Doris Lessing.

[28] Dale Peck, *Martin and John*, New York, Farrar Strauss Giroux, 1993.

onto a range of endings and, consequently, of diverse, compossible narratives. That same principle of star-shaping, playing on the multiple solutions offered by the combination of episodes, structures the participative narratives like video games, or hypertexual fictions calling for the internet users to do a *capricious* consultation (capricious etymologically echoing from "capra", goat in Latin, the jumping moves of the goat), by leaps from page to page, while choosing among the various possible links. More clearly still than in the texts which try to make the readers aware of their active role in the creation of the text, the process hands over part of the control function (here the laying down of an order), usually assigned to the narrator. And it can also be interpreted as another way to present a kind of authorial hesitation, by multiplying, like the publication of first drafts, the possible variants for the text. In all cases, the narration becomes multiplication and variation, and it gets closer that way to the practice of remakes, which obviously places the repeat of existing plots in a position of competition with the original, even when the intervention is minimal, as in Douglas Gordon's *24 hour Psycho* (1993), that is, limited to slowing down Hitchcock's film until its projection is extended to twenty-four hours—an effective way to submit it to an interrupted consumption, comparable to the one we have evoked concerning artist's videos.

Faced with that type of narratives, other authors seem to let the constraint of interruption play fully, either to favor forms of dense narration, similar, in that regard, to advertising narratives, or, on the opposite, to integrate the lack and the break extended into the heart of the discourse. Examples of the first case, the demands of publication in the press have imposed on American comics the format of the three box *strip,* a variant of short stories in three lines composed in the past by Félix Fénéon, and illustrated in works like Charles Schulz's *Peanuts,* or Bill Watterson's *Calvin and Hobbes*. An interesting phenomenon, the web comics, often published free of charge by their authors, alternate between that type of découpage, and the format of *graphic novels*, distilled to the rhythm of a few strips a week to a community of readers who, via some forum, can offer a comment on the evolution and thus offer the creators an immediate *feedback*, but also elaborate some *fanfictions*, changing into a collective scenarist—some sites even depending on a narrow dialogue with the readers invested with the task of deciding on the evolutions of a simple initial situation. The interruption in the publication permits then a debate between its various players which is reproduced, on the Internet, reminiscent to an increased degree, of the logic of some nineteenth century serialized novels. Opening and closing combine closely, a situation one finds in the blogs—those intimate/extimate writings, published on line, whose literary status is fluctuating, and which deliver to their readership some humorous notes, fictions or narratives (supposedly) autobiographical, and which are often indissociable from the forums commenting—and increasing—the textual offer, and making of the sites, again, a space for polyauthorial composition. Examples of the second case, some narrations have recourse, without hesitation, to amputation. David Foster Wallace gave an illustration of that in his cult novel, *Infinite jest*,[29] a romanesque leviathan of nearly a thousand pages (accompanied by a hundred pages of "notes and errata" where entire chapters, instructions on medicine use, or the filmography of one of the characters are given in a higgledy piggledy fashion) but which ends suddenly, with no resolution—at the same time by the interruption of the narrative, and because its plot revolves around a mythical film whose spectators would kill themselves, without its content ever being known. The desire for unity is therefore spoilt by the experience of a lack which can only appeal to the reader's imagination, both frustrated and invested with the power to finish the book as a co-narrator, or to read it again to find there some clues about the end, or some hidden elements. Contrary to Ricœur's hypotheses, the plotting here refuses to offer "an integrating dynamism which draws a story, whole and complete, from a set of separate accidents."[30]

Obviously, numerous other narrative modalities co-exist with the previous ones, each author playing at will on the whole range of possible forms.[31] At the heart of *Infinite jest,* the abundance of the voices, the presence of finished sub-narratives and the diversity of the treatments as of the subjects (from competitive tennis to advertising, from burlesque parody to romantic lyricism, from hard-boiled fiction to essays, from newspaper articles to information about dosage in medicines or to a film pitch) makes of that novel, in many different respects, a narration which remains integrating, in the sense that it gathers a real catalogue of available textualities. One simply wanted to underline how much the announced ending of a certain conception of the narrative is linked to a remarkable extension of the concept of narrativity, in a dialogue between the specifically artistic spheres and the other fields to be allotted to a narrative which, although self-critical, and submitting itself willingly to its own havoc, will not have ceased through that, to overflow, to go out of its presumed frames to explore its own ambiguities.

[29] David Foster Wallace, *Infinite jest*, Boston, Little, Brown & Co., 1995.

[30] Paul Ricœur, *Temps et récit, II: La Configuration dans le récit de fiction*, Paris, Seuil, 1984, p. 18 (see the critical comment that Viviane Asselin makes on that formula in the article quoted).

[31] For a panorama on that diversity in literature, see for example, Bruno Blanckeman, Aline Mura-Brunel and Marc Dambre dir., *Le Roman français au tournant du XXI*e *siècle*, Paris, Presses de la Sorbonne nouvelle, 2004.

BIBLIOGRAPHIC REFERENCES

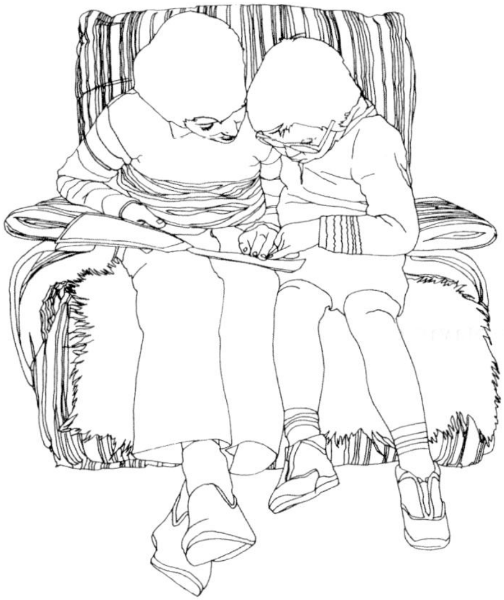

Je sentais..., Virginie Barré, 2004, mural - Courtesy galerie Loevebruck, Paris.

René Audet: ***Narrativity: away from story, close to eventness***

Adam, Jean-Michel (2001), *Les textes: types et prototypes: récit, description, argumentation, explication et dialogue*, Paris, Nathan Université (coll. "Fac Linguistique").

Armantier, Louis (1986), *Dictionnaire de la théorie et de l'histoire littéraires du XIXe siècle à nos jours*, Paris, Retz.

Audet, René (2006), "La fiction au péril du récit? Prolégomènes à une étude de la dialectique entre narrativité et fictionnalité", *Protée. Revue internationale de théories et de pratiques sémiotiques*, vol. 34, n° 2-3 (autumn-winter 2006-2007), p.193-207.

Audet, René, and Thierry Bissonnette (2004), "Le recueil littéraire, une variante formelle de la péripétie", *La narrativité contemporaine au Québec. 1. La littérature et ses enjeux narratifs*, edited by René Audet and Andrée Mercier, Québec, Presses de l'Université Laval, p.15-43.

Chevillard, Éric (2003), *Le vaillant petit tailleur*, Paris, Éditions de Minuit.

Cohen, Lynne, and Ann Thomas (2001), *No Man's Land. The Photography of Lynne Cohen,* London, Thames & Hudson. [I refer to two texts in that work: Ann Thomas, "Appropriating the Everyday", p. 9-21; "Camouflage": An Interview with Lynne Cohen" (interview between Lynne Cohen and William A. Ewing, Vincent Lavoie, Lori Pauli and Ann Thomas), p. 23-33.]

Farcy, Gérard-Denis (1991), *Lexique de la critique*, Paris, Presses universitaires de France.

Fludernik, Monika (2005), "Experientiality", *Routledge Encyclopedia of Narrative Theory*, edited by David Herman, Manfred Jahn and Marie-Laure Ryan, London and New York, Routledge, p.155.

Genette, Gérard (1972), *Figures III*, Paris, Éditions du Seuil (coll. "Poétique").

Greimas, Algirdas Julien, and Joseph Courtés (1979), *Sémiotique. Dictionnaire raisonné de la théorie du langage*, Paris, Hachette (coll. "Langue Linguistique Communication").

Herman, David (2002), *Story Logic. Problems and Possibilities of Narrative*, Lincoln and London, University of Nebraska Press (coll. "Frontiers of Narrative").

Herman, David (2005), "Events and Event-types", *Routledge Encyclopedia of Narrative Theory*, edited by David Herman, Manfred Jahn and Marie-Laure Ryan, London and New York, Routledge, p.151-152.

Joyce, Michael (1987), *Afternoon, a story*, Watertown (MA), Eastgate Systems (on disk).

Kore-eda, Hirokazu (2004), *Dare mo shiranai* [*Nobody Knows*], Japon, TV Man Union, Bandai Visual, Engine Film, c-style, Cine Qua Non, 135 mins.

Lotman, Iouri (1973), *La structure du texte artistique*, translated from the Russian by Anne Fournier, Bernard Kreise, Ève Malleret and Joëlle Yong, edited by Henri Meschonnic, Paris, Gallimard (coll. "Bibliothèque des sciences humaines").

Molino, Jean, and Raphaël Lafhail-Molino (2003), *Homo fabulator. Théorie et analyse du récit*, Arles / Montréal, Actes sud / Leméac.

Nuridsany, Claude, and Marie Pérennou (1996), *Microcosmos. Le peuple de l'herbe*, France-Suisse-Italie, Galatée Films, France 2 Cinéma, BAC Films, Delta Image, Les Productions JMH, TSR, Urania Films, Canal +, Conseil Général de l'Aveyron, Sivom des Monts et Lacs du Lévezou, CA, Région Midi-Pyrénées, CNC, Ministère de la Recherche and de l'Enseignement Supérieur, Agence Jules Verne, Office Fédéral de la Culture de Berne, Fondation GAN, Procirep, Fonds Eurimages, 80 mins.

Odin, Roger (2000), *De la fiction*, Bruxelles, De Boeck Université (coll. "Arts et cinéma").

Prince, Gerald ([1987] 2003), *A Dictionary of Narratology. Revised Edition*, Lincoln and London, University of Nebraska Press.

Prince, Gerald (1999), "Revisiting Narrativity", *Grenzüberschreitungen: Narratologie im Kontext / Transcending Boundaries: Narratology in Context*, edited by Walter Grünzweig and Andreas Solbach, Tübingen, Gunter Narr Verlag, p.43-51.

Prince, Gerald (2005), "Narrativity", *Routledge Encyclopedia of Narrative Theory*, edited by David Herman, Manfred Jahn and Marie-Laure Ryan, London and New York, Routledge, p.387-388.

Ricœur, Paul (1980), "Le récit de fiction", *La narrativité*, edited by Dorian Tiffeneau, Paris, Éditions du CNRS (coll. "Phénoménologie et herméneutique"), p.25-45.

Ricœur, Paul (1984), *Temps et récit. 2. La configuration du récit de fiction*, Paris, Éditions du Seuil (coll. "Points essais").

Romano, Claude (1999), *L'événement et le monde*, Paris, Presses universitaires de France (coll. "Épiméthée").

Ryan, Marie-Laure (1991), *Possible Worlds, Artificial Intelligence, and Narrative Theory*, Bloomington and Indianapolis, Indiana University Press.

Ryan, Marie-Laure (1992), "The modes of narrativity and their visual metaphors", *Style*, vol. 26, n° 3 (September), p.368-387.

Ryan, Marie-Laure (2005), "Narrative", *Routledge Encyclopedia of Narrative Theory*, edited by David

Herman, Manfred Jahn and Marie-Laure Ryan, London and New York, Routledge, p.344-348.
Ryan, Marie-Laure (2005), "Tellability", *Routledge Encyclopedia of Narrative Theory*, edited by David Herman, Manfred Jahn and Marie-Laure Ryan, London and New York, Routledge, p.589-591.
Viart, Dominique (1998), "Mémoires du récit. Questions à la modernité", *Mémoires du récit*, edited by Dominique Viart, Paris, Lettres modernes / Minard (coll. "Écritures contemporaines", 1), p.3-27.
Walker, Jill (1999), "Piecing apart and tearing together. Finding the story in *Afternoon*", *Proceedings of the tenth ACM Conference on Hypertext and Hypermedia: Returning to our diverse roots*, New York, ACM Press, p.111-117 (available online, *URL*: http://huminf.uib.no/~jill/txt/afternoon.html).

Carl Therrien: *Cinema under the influence of play*

Babeux, Sébastien (2004). *De la citation à l'interférence: croisements dans le film contemporain*, Montréal, Université de Montréal.
Bellour, Raymond (2004). "Le parti pris du réel", *Trafic*, n° 49, p. 5-13.
Benoliel, Bernard (1999). "Entretien avec Luc et Jean-Pierre Dardenne", *Cahiers du cinéma*, n° 539, october, p. 47-53.
Bordwell, David (1985). *Narration in the Fiction Film*, Madison, University of Wisconsin Press.
Céghin, Cyril (2005). "Cut-up en plein ciel", *Vertigo*, n° 27, march, p. 23-26.
Collectif (2002). "Hollywood Disaster, carnet de route. Dix virages sur 'Mulholland Drive'", *Vertigo*, hors-série, november, p. 66-77.
Eig, Jonathan (2003). "A beautiful mind(fuck): Hollywood structures of identity", *Jump Cut. A Review of Contemporary Media*, no 46, summer, pp. 38-53. [On-line]: <http://www.ejumpcut.org/archive/jc46.2003/eig.mindfilms/index.html>
Ferenczi, Aurélien (2000). "Sixième Sens", *Télérama*, n° 2608, 5 january, p. 28.
Gardies, André (1972). "Vers un mode de rapport nouveau avec le spectateur: le ludique", *Alain Robbe-Grillet*, Paris, Seghers, p. 93-102.
Gaudreault, André et François Jost (1990). *Le récit cinématographique*, Paris, Nathan.
Gauthier, Guy (1993). "Le jeu du retour et du hasard", conversation with Alain Resnais, *Le mensuel du cinéma*, n° 12, december, p. 62-67.
Greenaway, Peter (2006). "The Tulse Luper Suitcases" [on-line]: <http://petergreenaway.co.uk/tulse.htm>
Higuinen, Erwan, Charles Tesson (2002). "Jeux Vidéo. La nouvelle alliance du film et du jeu", *Cahiers du cinéma*, Dossier: Cinéma et jeux vidéo: les nouvelles correspondances, p. 10-11.
Ishaghpour, Youssef (1986). *Cinéma contemporain. De ce côté du miroir*, Paris, Éditions de la Différence.
Leutrat, Jean-Louis (2004). "No Smoking et Smoking. Hutton Buscel, ou bien... ou bien...", *Positif*, n° 395, january, p. 78-80.
Mandolini, Carlo (1999). "The Sixth Sense", *Séquences*, n° 205, november/december, p. 43.
Manovich, Lev (2001). *The Language of New Media*, Cambridge, The MIT Press.
Ostria, Vincent (1994). "Glissements progressifs du plaisir interactif", *Cahiers du cinéma*, n° 476, february, p. 65-68.
Perron, Bernard (1999). "Un indice pour ouvrir le jeu", in *Cinémas*, Vol. 10, n° 1, p. 93-110.
_____ (2004). "Plein jeux sur le cinéma contemporain", Actes du colloque *Cinéma contemporain, état des lieux* de Lyon, 2002 (sous la direction de Jean-Pierre Esquenazi), Paris, L'Harmattan, p. 293-308.
_____ (2005). "L'approche ludique du cinéma de fiction: un jeu à motif mixte", *Culture médiatique*, vol. 2, "Compar(a)ison" , p. 69 to 88.
Prince, Gerald (2003). *Dictionary of Narratology. Revised Edition*, Lincoln, University of Nebraska Press.
Ricœur, Paul (1983). *Temps et récit. Tome I*, Paris, Éditions du Seuil.
_____ (1984). *Temps et récit II. La configuration du temps dans le récit de fiction*, Paris, Éditions du Seuil.
Rigoulet, Laurent (2003). "Ados à bout portant", conversation with Gus Van Sant, *Télérama*, n° 2806, 22 october, p. 14-20.
Ruiz, Raoul (1995). *Poétique du cinéma*, Paris, Dis Voir.
Valletoux, Thierry (1995). "Le cinéma dans l'enfer du jeu", *Studio*, Dossier spécial jeu vidéo, n° 104, november, p. 116-121.

Printed by
POLICROM
Barcelona - Spain
February 2007